大展好書　好書大展
品嘗好書　冠群可期

大展好書　好書大展

品嘗好書· 冠群可期

盧式
心意六合拳
開 拳

附VCD

Lu Style Xinyi Liuhe Quan Intermediate

余 江 著
Author Jiang Yu

孫慧敏 姜淑霞 翻譯
Translated by Huimin Sun, Shuxia Jiang

王書文 顧問

大展出版社有限公司

感　謝

　　這一套介紹盧式心意六合拳的書，雖然由我執筆完稿，其實可說是集體智慧的結晶，一是繼承王書文老師及前輩們經驗的傳授，二是這些年與眾師兄弟們無間交流的成果，書中的某些段落文字還仗著有宿琳、王周、吳秋亭、譚全勝老師們的無私提供。

　　感謝盧少君師叔在病危中爲本書提詞。感謝這些年常在一道打拳、喝茶的蔡泊澄、薛鴻恩、李傳鄉、錢仁表、唐毓堃、張岳定、孫雙喜等師兄們。感謝遠在加拿大的胡剛兄百忙中爲本書寫序。

余　江

盧式心意六合拳開拳

Special Thanks

Although this book was finished a piece of writing by me to introduce Lu Style Xinyi Liuhe Quan, actually it was a collective intelligence, one part came from Master Shuwen Wang and many predecessors 'impart, the other is the result of interflow between me and many fellow apprentices of one and the same master, some words in this book were provided selflessly by Master Lin Su, Master Zhou Wang, Master Qiuting Wu, and Master Quansheng Tan.

I special appreciate for Master Shaojun Lu writes the inscription when he was critically ill. And many thanks for Bocheng Cai, Hongen Xue, Chuanxiang Li, Renbiao Qian, Yukun Tang, Yueding Zhang, Shuangxi Sun. They practice with me frequently in these years. Thanks Gang Hu in Canada wrote me the preface although he is very busy.

Jiang Yu

一代宗師盧嵩高像
The picture of Master Songgao Lu

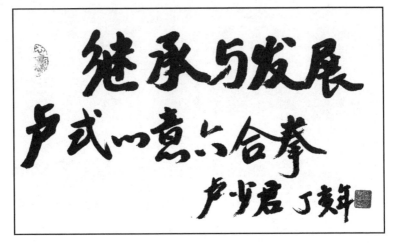

Inheritance and development Lu Style Xinyi Liuhe Quan
Shaojun Lu

註：盧少君老師爲盧嵩高之子

Note: Master Shaojun Lu is the son of Songgao Lu

為盧式心意著作序

中華文化博大精深，絕非虛語。其一為文，其二曰武，其三不計其數。

文之證據：

三墳、五典、八索、九丘、詩經、諸子、楚辭、漢賦、樂府、唐詩、宋詞、元曲、明清小說、民國白話，聖跡無度，一貫法書。

武之實驗：

七經典武，計謀贏輸；千年秦劍，寒光發怵；朝改代換，長城具睹，金戈鐵馬，成敗不素；內外各族，幾度征服；戰例難數，殘陽月渡；英雄輩出，血雨江湖；民間武林，門派奇數；鄉間村落，高手頻步；北少南武，中南山柱；豪傑無數，把把拳術；地球萬載，此景誰住？

回首武林一片，心意六合閃亮武林幾百年。以根源而論，發之於黃河，遠不說宋代岳武穆英雄一世，就明末至清中，姬龍鳳、曹繼武、馬學禮、戴龍邦、金一望各先祖及傳人，躍於黃河兩岸，威風席捲中原大地一片；民國時期，原傳一支寶鼎，盧嵩高、尚學禮、宋國賓、范百川諸前輩，引其入長江大流域，風起雲湧武林知。以朝代時局論，心意拳演變分支現，竟與中國命運一一大相息！今上海推出盧式心意拳，對應何？原來是華夏文化復興大時機！

六合心意一脈，何至於此，主根不變，支支變，卻與中國命運環環相扣、節節緊密連？蓋其文化之深也！ 何其深？不可深問焉！留於近日見分曉！

蓋其技術之精也！何其精？不可喻也！空口無憑，留待各位去驗體。

武師風範，盧氏諸公，武藝文獻皆傳授，更有拳譜定乾坤，佐證河南山西六合文！

文士雅儒，余江諸位，事業生活兩成功；繼承發展都不誤，分享深度樂趣於社會；忽發好術於此書，按部就班人人知，何其幸?！心意上海幾老：王、凌、李、于諸公在其中！

黃河、長江、海洋大融流，時光匆匆；名利無邊，體有限，留與少許於心意，回報定不已！

勉為序！

胡剛於加拿大首府渥汰華探微齋

Introduction of Lu Style Xinyi

The Chinese culture is extensive and profound, and includes literary and martial arts.

The example of the martial art: the classic seven books of martial arts (Wu Jin Qi Shu) for wars. The ancient sword made thousands of years ago in Qin Dynasty still shines.

How many dynasties were replaced? The Great Wall knows. The shining spears and armored horses, no matter victorious or defeated, all bled. Some ethnic groups made conquests both within and without.

How many battles were fought? Only the sun and the moon know. Heroes appeared one after another, from the blood competitions in the old times of China.

Many styles of the martial arts exist in Chinese Wushu society. Even in countryside, there are many masters.

The famous martial arts which are related to the mountains are Shaolin (originated from Shong Mountain) in north, Wudang (originated from Wudang Mountain) in South and Xinyi Quan (originated from Zhongnan Mountain) in the middle.

Heroes, who have their own styles of martial arts, are countless. For thousands of years on the earth, who owns these but China?

When you recall the history of martial arts in China, Xinyi Liuhe Quan has shined in the Wushu society for hundreds years.

Xinyi Liuhe Quan originated from the Yellow River. Even without mentioning the Song Dynasty's hero Yue Fei, there are still Master Longfeng Ji, Jiwu Cao, Xueli Ma, Longbang Dai and Yiwang Jing from the Ming Dynasty and in the middle of the Qing Dynasty, as well as other disciples, spread across the nation and known by both sides of the Yellow River, their power and prestige sweeping the Central Plains.

At the beginning of the last century, the masters such as Mr. Songgao Lu, Xueli Shang, Guobin Song, Baichuan Fan etc. brought Xinyi from the Yellow River to the area of Changjiang River (the Yangtse River), and to the attention of everyone in the Chinese martial arts society.

When we trace back, we are surprised to find that the changes in Xinyi Quan reflect many historical changes in China.

What Lu Style Xinyi is reflecting today? It is reflecting the revival of Chinese culture today!

Why does Liuhe Xinyi have this connection to Chinese history? First, it is because the culture is profound. How profound?

為盧式心意著作序

You will discover for yourself very soon. Second, it is that the techniques are excellent. How excellent? There are no words to describe their excellence; the readers will realize through practice.

The styles of Mr. Lu and the other masters have not only taught the techniques, but also left the Quan Pu (book of theory) to their students. For example, the Quan Pu of Liu He Quan left by Master Lu gave a solid foundation to the Shanghai Xinyi, which also proved that the preface in the Liuhe Quan kept in Shanxi is real.

Mr Jiang Yu and others are not only successful in business but also in life; not only have they inherited Xinyi Quan, but they have also improved and shared it with the society.

Today, they will publish the book on Lu Style Xinyi, and how lucky the readers are to follow their steps to learn Lu Style Xinyi!

How lucky the senior masters (over 80 years old) Li, Wang, Lin and Yu are to be involved too!

The Yellow River, Changjiang River, and the oceans are interflowing; time is flying by, fame and fortune are endless, but not life. Why not leave some time to practice Xinyi and be rewarded with a better health?

Preface by Hugang
Ottawa, the capital of Canada

開 學 導 語

　　盧式心意，又有人稱：上海十大形，模仿十種動物：雞、鷂、燕、鷹、虎、馬、熊、蛇、猴、龍，似十種人形 —— 高、矮、胖、瘦、甲、由、目、申、干、虛。

　　你不必依本書十形的順序來開拳，而是要先認清自己，似熊、似猴、似虎、似蛇……擇一形來開拳，因人而異，時間長了，功夫長了，做到十形合一（指十大動物之形意）。

　　盧式心意歷來傳拳都少在公開場所，而是單個在師父的家中傳拳、演拳、喝茶，而且每個人開拳的動作還都不一樣，各有側重，規定師兄弟間也少要竄拳，道理就在於師父要做到因材施教。

　　由外入內，由糾正拳架的規整、合順運動軌跡的合理開始，從四梢中的肉梢開始，拳打千萬次，能做到熟能生巧，肌肉有記憶力，動作才能做到合理、合順，爾後開始練習四梢中的筋梢、骨梢，使在打拳的過程中學會應用筋骨的力量。這在開拳（中級）階段。

　　幾年可以出師？技術上套用八個字來說：有用、好用、妙用、大用。

　　有用者三個月。新兵訓練三個月，就可以上戰場。盧式心意也一樣，「十年××不出門，三個月心意打壞人。」入門六式加四炮，勤盤三月，拳打萬遍，幾次對抗，一勇二膽三功夫，三個月足矣。

　　好用者得一年或半載。熟練掌握盧式心意入門和開拳階段的技術，得意於盧式心意某一、二個形的動作，不怕千招會，只怕一招精，用的好誰都會讓你三分。因為工作、生活等原因，諸多前輩未能深入學習下去，但好用好使，是盧式心意現在最多的人群。

　　知妙用者須勤練三年。是盧式心意入室弟子，掌握盧式心意的技術要求，懂得盧式心意的技術奧妙，心明身行，入得了形、相，知變化。

　　有大用者至少得用六年。通曉盧式心意，說得清、道得明，有形有意，就可以出師了，農耕社會，可以聞名方圓百里，算得上名家明師了。

　　馬學禮學藝六年，李洛能好像也是學藝六年，他們皆是比我們專心用功。

　　至於孤獨求藝，一心一意或無心無意，我說不清了。

Instruction

Lu Style Xinyi is also named Shanghai Ten Big Forms, imitating the movements of ten types of animals: Rooster, Hawk, Swallow, Eagle, Tiger, Horse, Bear, Snake, Monkey and Dragon, and representing 10 human body shapes, such as Tall, Short, Fat, Thin and so on. It is not necessary to practice them in the order that is described in this book. You can choose one that most suits you and start with it. By persistently practicing the forms one by one, you can unify their strength into one.

Lu Style Xinyi is seldom taught in public classes. The masters usually teach, practice, and drink tea at home with their students individually. According the individual's abilities, they are arranged with different beginning forms.

The practice begins from the correct stance and the movements, from outside to inside, from the ends of muscles. To practice them thousands of times, build them first into the muscles, then into the end of the tendons, and the end of the bones. During training, learn to use the power of the tendons and bones and your studies will reach the middle level.

How long is needed to finish the study? Technically, it can be either useful, good, skillful, or outstanding.

If you want it to be useful, three months should be enough, just like that a recruit can be sent to a battle after three-months training. Lu Style Xinyi is the same as the saying "Three months on Xinyi better than 10 years on something else". To practice the basic six forms and the four Cannon Fists again and again, within three months you would have the courage, the boldness, and the skills to face your opponent. If you want to be good at it, then one year and a half would be necessary. Try to master the basic techniques of Lu Style Xinyi and deeply understand the essence of the movements of one or two forms named by the ten animals. You do not have to know many forms, and using one form well, anyone would try to avoid you. For many reasons, some people stay at this stage and do not probe further into Lu Style Xinyi, but it can still be very useful.

To be skillful, three years of hard work is needed. You have to be admitted as a disciple of Lu Style Xinyi and have mastered the essential techniques; you should not only be able to lead the body to follow the mind, but also be capable of making changes between the various forms freely. To be outstanding, at least six years of practice should be arranged. To fully understand Lu Style Xinyi means that you must know why and how to perform the arts, and unify the forms and the mind. And your study is finished . At that time, you would be well known within hundreds of miles and also treated as a great master. Xueli Ma and Luoneng Li both had learnt XinYi for six years. They were much more concentrated and diligent than we are.

To reach the highest level of the martial art, depends on an individual's ability and effort.

目　錄

Table of Contents

盧式心意・風采

The Elegancy of Lu Style Xinyi Quan

一、軍事用武的典範

盧式心意的血脈之本一是千百年來軍隊用武的延續。兩兵相對，驚心動魄，敵我相視，先有殺敵之心，後有動手之意，古來這叫一心一意。驚心之事要心神專注，含得住一口氣，沉得了一顆心，內三合使人神不斷，外三合使人形不散，永遠是以中正之氣罩著你，像上了膛的槍一樣瞄著你，上下束一，不動則已，放膽一決，動則必靈。「不動如山岳，難知如陰陽，無窮如天地，浩渺如四海，眩耀如電光；盡乎其智，備乎其勇，全乎其和……」

心意拳長時間以來是一門秘不外傳的拳術，只在軍隊中流傳，掌握在將軍、總兵等上層軍士的手裡，為了防止被人偷學，仿效了舊時對軍隊的管理辦法，練兵的不帶兵，帶兵的人不練兵，把心意六合拳一裁為二，「盤法歸盤法，用法歸用法，盤而不能用」，並在拳譜中規定：

心意六合不亂傳，多少奧妙在其間；

若教枉徒無義漢，招災惹禍保身難；

君子學了護終生，小人學了胡亂傳；

背後莫談旁人短，遇事莫要強出頭；

山上石多黃金稀，路上人多君子少；

寧可失傳，不可亂傳。

新兵蛋子，勇敢；老兵油子，狡猾。知合順者長壽，知順受者長命，知六合者知存有餘地，留有變化。知心意者知生死之術。兩兵相對勇者勝，硬打硬上無遮攔，一勇、二膽、三功夫。兩勇相持智者勝，迎打攔上無遮攔，知無變化者不打人，以正迎之以奇勝。兩智相見視死者生，破釜沉舟，有絕死之心，才決勁。

盧式心意勁練五決：踩、撲、裹、束、決，踩要決，撲要決，裹要決，束要決，決要決，堅決執行，絕地而決，如洪之下瀉，石之滾落，無人敢接，無人敢擋。拳出不空回，令出如山倒，寫到此，我彷彿聽到了衝鋒的號角，雷鼓喧天，千萬人衝將出去，不計身家性命，忘形、得意、一心，不勝利不回頭。

1. A model of the application of martial arts in the military

One branch of Lu Style Xinyi Quan came from the way armies were trained for thousands of years. When the opponents confronted each other on the battlefield, a soul-stirring moment, the emotional mind of killing was aroused first, the determination of acting then followed. This is just what we called "the heart (Xin) and the mind (Yi)". To forestall the antagonist, one has to concentrate his mind and keep calm for the action;

Three Internal Harmonies help one keep his spirit ceaselessly and Three External Harmonies keep the movements integrated. Always with the overawing power of righteousness and the accuracy of a shot, as long as the action is taken, it will surely succeed.

Just as the verses said "calm as a mountain, unpredictable as Yin and Yang, unlimited as the sky and the earth, vast like the ocean, bright as the lightening; being full of wisdom, courage and harmony……" Xinyi Quan had ever been imparted inside the military for a long time, but only the marshals and the high level officers mastered the techniques. Lest the skill be betrayed to others, they adopted the imperial management used in the past to control the army: those who train the soldiers are not the ones who command them, and those who govern the soldiers are not the ones who train them. They divided the Xinyi Quan into two parts: one for exercise and another for use. "What is learned in exercises is different in practice" and set the rules:

Do not pass the skill to a random person; there is much mystery hidden inside.

If it is learnt by a villain, great trouble could be made for you;

An honorable man uses it for a good use, while a small man just shows off around;

Do not talk to people on their backs, and never show eagerly at conflict;

Stones are more than gold in the mountain, less honor men in the crowd on the road;

It would be better to fail to hand down the techniques than to have them fall into the wrong hands.

A recruit is brave; a veteran is tactful. The one who treasures peace enjoys longevity; the one who endures hardships survives; the one who understands the Six Harmonies leaves space for return; the one who comprehends Xin (heart) and Yi (mind) possesses the key for life. When two opposing armies meet on the battlefield, the braver wins. Fight hard and no one can stop. One needs first, bravery, second, boldness, and third, techniques. When two brave opposites meet, the wiser wins. Beat directly in a twisted way and no one can block. Do not fight, if you do not know changes. Clinch a victory with an unexpected way. When two wise opposites meet, the one who fights desperately survives; the one who breaks the caldrons, sinks the boat, and uses all his power with no fear of death wins. Lu Style Xinyi Quan emphasizes the Five Actions: Stamp (Cai), Pounce (Pu), Wrap (Guo), Bind (Su) and Burst (Jue). Stamp to the utmost; Pounce to the utmost, Enwrap to the utmost, Burst to the utmost. Act fast, determinedly, as if a flood rushing or stones rolling down from a hill, no one dares to stand in the way. Fists never go empty and commands are as if mountains falling down. It seems like bugles and drums buzzing in the sky, soldiers are marching forward, totally forgetting themselves, only one aim in their mind: the victory. No victory, no return.

二、海派武文化

盧式心意的血脈之本二是都市武文化性，是優秀的海派武文化。具有大都市的人文氣質與人文精神，是流傳千年的黃河文明與海派文化的融成，以人為本，適時適下，不斷取法。都市也同時賦予了盧式心意更多的現代性、城市性，「海納百川，有融乃大」是我們的活水源。

正是這些文化的魅力吸引了代代愛好者來細緻玩味，格物深究。

1. 方寸之地，可以打拳，不受空間限制

城市裡寸土寸金，上海人家中三世同堂不少（過去），人均八個平方。盧式心意一床之地就可以打拳，弄堂裡可以打拳，公園裡可以打拳，馬路邊可以打拳，直道可以打拳。

盧式心意歷來傳拳多在師父的家裡，四方之地、

十多個平方，有床、有桌、有家，好幾個師兄弟，轉身之地，教的盡心、學的盡興，不顯小。

2. 隨手之時，可以打拳，不受時間限制

城市人，時間是金錢、效益，一寸光陰一寸金，寸金難買寸光陰。盧式心意打拳的方法是單操多盤，熟能生巧，以一貫十，隨手打拳，不受時間的限制。千招會不如一招精，合適之所，三五分鐘即可打拳，貴在狀態，每天有幾個三五分鐘，分而打之就會有進步。我常在上下班的路上打拳，暗晃中節，暗溜雞腿，公車上暗站椿，行人只會稍感異樣，不會在意。我也常在開會與開會間、接待與等待間打拳，興致所來，隨手打之，聞敲門聲止，一臉的微笑，滿面的紅光，常被人誇獎，氣色不錯。

每天若有三十分鐘左右的時間打拳，日就月將必有所成，因為他的拳性是短而促，凶而勇，如咆哮之水東來，滾落之石天落，見心、見勢、見勇。有時間，打拳一次在六十分鐘以上時，要打拳入味，用意不用力，不是每把都要見勢見勇，而是要細而用心地玩味，注意細節，心意束一。

3. 老少皆宜，都可打拳，不受年齡限制

少來打拳，強身健體，保命保家保生活；

老來打拳，修身養性，養功養道養天真。

盧師常講：「咱這一門拳是枯枝梅，沒有葉只有

花，不好看，中用，是制人的拳。」。學拳時要有一定的力量基礎和一定的理解能力，明白道理就容易入門，所以年齡最好在17歲至45歲間，內外兼修，剛柔相濟。

少年打拳要多盤技術，少練功，功要隨著身體的長成而加強。老來打拳，也是拳拳見心，但心不同，要多練形於內，用意不用力，同樣的動作，同樣一把拳，因目的不同，要求不同。

「靜養靈根氣養神，養功養道見天真。」日就月將，老樹會發新芽，如有新生。

2. The Martial Arts Culture of Shanghai Style

The second branch of Lu Style Xinyi Quan is the feature of the metropolis, which is the culture of the Shanghai Style martial arts. It carries the qualities and the spirit of humanity, composing the Yellow River's civilization and the traditional culture of Shanghai. With the purpose of building up the human being's body and spirit, it has been developed with time and kept learning from its environment. Meanwhile, the city also bestows on it more modernity and urbanity.

As the Sea accommodates the torrents from thousands of rivers, the excellence of Xinyi attracts many generations of enthusiasts to work on its profundity.

(1) Not Limited by Space

Space has always been a problem in cities. In the past, three generations living in the same house was normal in Shanghai. It is about 8 square meters per person. Yet, Lu Style Xinyi can be performed in a space that is the same size as a bed. One can practice it in a passageway or a park, or by the side of a street. Traditionally, the masters taught Lu Style Xinyi at home, usually in a room of about ten square meters with a bed, a table and other furniture. Even so, the master and students did their best to teach and learn, and enjoyed themselves.

(2) No time limitation

For the people living in a big city, time means money and benefit, as the old proverb said: "one inch of time worth one inch of gold, but one inch of gold can not buy one inch of time". One method to learn Lu Style Xinyi is to practice a single form many times. Practice makes it perfect and use it against ten. Practicing it at any time, it is not limited by time.

It is believed that to learn a thousand skills superficially is not as good as to learn one skill thoroughly. At an appropriate place, even a span of three or five minutes can be used to practice Xinyi, if you feel good. Every day, if you use several 3- minutes or 5- minutes, you'll surely make progress. I used to do it myself on the way going to work and the way back home. I shook my middle section or practiced "Chicken Slip", or practiced "Stances" (Zan Zhuang) in the buses. The people around might think it was a little odd, but they did not really care. I also did it at the break of meetings, or during a waiting time, depending on the mood.

If some knocked the door at the moment, they would find me having a ruddy complexion and praise me of good spirit. If one practices Xinyi for 30 minutes every day, he will be assured of achieving something. His fists must be short and speedy, fierce and powerful, just like the roaring water flowing to the east and the rolling stone falling down from the air, with determination, power and brave. However, if one has the time to practice Xinyi Quan for more than an hour at a time, he should pay more attention on the mind, not just the force. Pay more attention not only to the power and courage in every movement, but also to the understanding of the motion and details, and unifying the mind and heart.

(3) It suites all ages

A youth can use Xinyi to build up his body and to protect his life and family;

An elder can use Xinyi to improve his health and cultivate his nature, skills, and simplicity of his life.

Master Lu often said: Lu style of Xinyi Quan is like a flower tree with only flowers but no leaves. It is not good for viewing but good for use. It is really effective to win the fight. One must have certain strength and ability to start with, and to understand the principles first would be a great help for beginners. The age of the beginner is best around 17 to 45. They should be trained both externally and internally, and also the softness with the hardness.

A youngster should pay more attention to the techniques rather than to Gong Fu (internal energy), for Gong Fu will enhance with the body growing up. An elder should pay more attention on the heart and spend more time on internal practicing and use the mind rather than the force. Depending on different purposes, there could be different requirements on the same movement.

"Quietness cultivates the root of the soul and Qi (internal energy) nourishes the spirit. Cultivate Gong Fu and morality to see the truth. Day by day and month by month, as if an old tree sprouts, the elder will feel refreshed.

三、修身・洗性・長命

盧式心意的血脈之本三是長生性，是千百年來人們追求長命百歲經驗歷程的結晶。時值當下在上海的武術界，有六位九十歲以上高齡仍在行拳授課的知名武林老壽星，全都是盧式心意門的。

　　白雲飛老師九十有六，還有王書文老師、李尊思老師、凌漢興老師、於化龍老師和王多鳳老師。王多鳳老師，女，九十多歲仍參加2008年第九屆上海國際武術博覽會首屆武穆杯心意六合拳的名家表演，精神飽滿，出拳有力。

　　心意拳史上諸多老師都很長壽，具有普遍性，這種長生性是拳性所為。

　　人常說：命不可改，運可以籌。人的遺傳基因不可改，但因為後天不良習氣，所形成的毛病是可以修正、洗清的。這種不良習氣多從少年時開始，自己又不注意。如坐姿的不正確、飲食的不合理、生活的不規律，直接導致步入中年後的一身毛病，老年時的一生痛苦。

　　病痛積苦貴在有先知先覺，在中青年時透過鍛鍊來修正、洗清，學習盧式心意是最好的方法之一。

　　聽天由命是因緣，看你的造化；自作自受是因果，看你的態度。

　　人一血肉之軀，外應筋骨皮，內對五臟六腑，內外相繫呼吸二字。「外似山，內如水，呼吸是藍天，想要好、梢中求，方知靈山大光明。」筋骨皮可以用修身的方法糾正，五臟六腑可以用洗性的方法來改良，以舊換新，叫：易，所以又稱：易肌、易筋、易骨、易髓、易內腑……聽起來很複雜，其實很簡單。

　　打一比喻，人像是一座現代建築，骨就是建築中的框架，如鋼架、橋樑；筋在建築中的作用是連結，如纜繩；肉是建築中的外飾，如水泥、紅磚。常言道：骨不好了，用筋來糾；筋骨不好了，水泥要厚一些。盧式心意多講四梢，部分道理就在這裡。

　　修身，一是在日常生活中透過培養正確的坐姿、站姿、走姿來糾正；二是在打拳的過程中透過長肌、伸筋、拔骨等方法修正。

　　修身首要正骨，測定的方法是哪沾哪實、哪受力哪痛，而不能是其他部位。如：正確的坐姿，保持盧式心意身成六勢中對上半身的要求，屁股沾實凳子，時間長了屁股痛是對的，而不應該是腰痛、頸痛。正確的站姿，站的時間長了腳底板痛是對的。走也是這樣，學習盧式心意中溜雞腿與踩雞步，保持盧式心意中身成六勢的要求，腳底沾實，時間長了腳底板痛是對的，其他任何一處疼痛都是不正確的，如膝痛、腰痛………膝痛腰傷是拳架不正的標誌。

　　伸筋：你可以在打拳的過程中透過撐、拔、伸、擰來練習，也可以直接練習盧式心意易筋十三式。長肌：在打拳的過程中長肌是最合理的，需要哪一塊，增長那一塊，過了反到不好。

　　人的心肺功能有限，一定要轎車的動力帶一輛卡車跑，不累死也得喘。

　　洗性：中國人講：性相近，習相遠，習慣的良否決定內腑的健康，內腑的健康決定性情的好惡，性情的累積影響性格。內腑堅實，功能才良好，才能叫健康，人才能有精神，有了精神才能有好的性情，做事、打拳才能有旺盛的精力。

　　洗性二字也可以講精神二字，也可以說是內臟的健康。內臟的健康源於氣血的旺盛與否，氣血循環的通暢與否，氣血運動的方式合理與否。

　　洗性一如水之洗衣。四梢中血梢，外達於髮，內循於裡，痛則不通，通則不痛，生津化淤。洗性有兩種辦法，一是由外導內；二是以內引內。盧式心意主張內外兼修。

　　起源於黃河岸邊的心意六合拳和融成於浦江兩岸的盧式心意六合拳，行拳如水之漫延，緩若浩渺如水之湧來湧去，動如奔騰如水之咆哮，拳勢洶湧有節，內勢鼓蕩有律，拳性似水，水的潮起潮落之勢合乎於天地之律。人要依勢洗性，而不是依式洗性。

　　盧式心意打拳的方法就是「直立行走」，蹲直與頂直。人體的構架最適合於直立行走，走的節律最合於氣血的節律，如水之東來拍岸，往左、往前、往右，不回頭。拳譜曰：前有三條路，往左、往前、往右，不回頭。

　　盧式心意另傳有內功十三篇，年長的愛好者始於以內養內、引內，然後內外兼修，依法練習。長命，就是依律有節的涵養，不過分，盈。

3. Health Benefiting, Spirit Growing, Life Prolonging

The third branch of Lu style Xinyi is its benefit for life prolongation. It is the result of the experience coming from the efforts of human beings pursuing longevity for thousands of years. Currently in Shanghai's Wushu circle, there are six famous masters of Xinyi who are still undertaking the work of training and teaching.

They are Mr. Bai Yunfei (96 years old), Mr. Wan Shuwen, Mr. Li Zunsi, Mr. Ling Hanxing, Mr. Yu Hualong and Ms. Wang Duofeng. Ms. Wang Duofeng, even though over ninety years old, made excellent performance at the first Wumu Cup competition, in the Ninth Shanghai International Wushu Fair 2008. In Xinyi history, many maters enjoyed their longevity, which has sufficiently shown the style's distinguished quality.

People usually say that one's fortune can be changed while one's fate is destined. Even though one's genes are settled, his habit and shortcoming can still be corrected. These bad habits, such as a bad sitting posture, a wrong diet or an irregular living style, which might have been fostered since one's childhood, may probably cause some illness at middle age and suffering later. It is important to foresee it. To practice Xinyi since young age is one of the best ways to prevent some illness.

Something is destined, that is your fate; something is the result of what you have done, that depends on your attitude.

A human body has tendons, bones, and skin, and also organs inside. The inside and outside are connected by breathing. It was described as "the outside is like a mountain and the inside like water, breath like the sky. If you want to do the best, make efforts on the ends, and then you will find the great sunshine on the spirit mountain". The tendons, bones, and skin can be strengthened through exercising and the function of the organs can be improved by cultivating nature. To change the old for the new is called "Yi" (易) in Chinese. So, we have "Yi Ji" (Muscles Changing), "Yi Jin" (Tendons Changing), "Yi Gu" (Bones Changing), "Yi Sui" (Marrows Changing), "Yi Neifu" (Viscera Changing) ---- these concepts sound complicated, but are actually simple.

To explain this, we can compare the human body as a modern building; the bones are the frame of the building, like structures and bridges; the tendons are the connection, like cables; the muscles are the decoration outside the building, like concrete and bricks. As the proverb said: "if bones are impaired, use tendons to compensate; if tendons are weakened, use more concrete". This is why Lu Style Xinyi talks more about the four ends.

To cultivate your body (Xiu Shen), first, is to sit, stand, and walk in a right way; second, to grow muscles, stretch tendons and bones during exercises.

The most important thing to do is to place the bones in right positions. Whether the bones are at the right state, can be tested it by feeling it. If the part that burdens the force feels pain, not some other parts, that means it is OK.

For example, if you sit for a long time, you should feel uncomfortable at the buttocks, not the waist or the neck; if you walk long, you should feel pain at the soles of the feet. When you practice the Chicken Leg or Chicken Step, try to meet the requirements of Lu Style Xinyi and maintain the Six Body Postures, if you stand solid on the ground long, it is all right that the soles of your feet feel pain. Contrastingly, it will be not good if other parts of your body, such as the knees or waist feel wrong, which means that your stance is incorrect.

Stretching tendons: it can be achieved by supporting, pulling, extending, and twisting in the exercises. You can also practice Lu Style Xinyi Thirteen Forms of Changing Tendons for the same purpose. Muscle growth is a natural result of practicing. Train the parts where the muscles need to be improved, not other parts. The capacity of the heart and lung is limited. As if the energy of a car is not enough for a truck to run, one should not overdo the training.

To cultivate your characters (Xi Xing): There is a Chinese saying: "human natures are born to be similar, but the habits drive them apart". Good habits bring healthy organs, which also impact one's temperament. And the temperament accumulates to form one's character.

Only when a person's organs are in good condition and function well, he can have a healthy spirit, which in turn rewards him with a nice personality, and then he is vigorous in working and exercise. Therefore, to cultivate one's characters is relevant to one's spirit and health. The healthy organs depend on sufficient blood and internal energy (Qi), which come from the fluency of their circulation and reasonable exercises.

Cultivate your character as if washing a cloth with water. In the four ends, the end of blood reaches the hair outside and circulates inside, promoting the secretion of saliva and removes blood stasis. If one feels pain, the circulation must be blocked; if the circulation is fluent, one will not feel pain. There are two methods to cultivate your character: first, use the outside to lead the inside; second, use the inside to lead the inside. Lu Style Xinyi advocates developing both ways at the same time.

Xinyi Liu He Quan rooted in Huanghe (Yellow River) area and Lu Style Xinyi Liu He Quan from Pujiang (Pu River) area both have the same water—like quality, slow as a wave surging forward or backward; dynamic like water rolling over. The power of its motion gallops with control, like the tide up and down, following the rules of nature. A person should develop his mind according the laws of nature rather than any man—made regulations.

The method of practicing Lu Style Xinyi Quan is "while walking, keep the upper body and the head upright", so does the squat or stance, which are suitable for the structure of a human body. The rate of walking applies to the rate of Qi and blood, as if the water flows to the east shore, leftward, forward, rightward, but not backward. A verse said: "there are three roads ahead: left, forth, and right, but no turning back.

Lu Style Xinyi has another thirteen chapters on internal martial arts. Senior enthusiasts can start first from the method of building the inside and then develop both outside and inside. Longevity comes from following the rules of nature and avoids overdoing.

四、盧師基因

盧師已經離開我們快五十年了，今人現還無一有超越，無論從德行上、技術上。常聽圈內圈外人講盧師，也常對別人講盧師，感覺盧師就在我們身邊，彷彿可以聽見他說，看見他演拳似的。

盧師一生坎坷蹉跎，家境貧寒，不識字，只會寫自己的名字，只會一心一意打自己的拳，既不是第一也不是最後一位來滬的武術老師。百餘年來只有盧師在上海開創了武術一派之先河，成就了一代武林宗師的崇高地位，並功成身退在上海。

盧師一生勤奮，善交流，多實踐，不成見，好思考，善融通。盧師好學，不墨守陳規，而是開創性地繼承，邊學習邊實踐，邊思考邊改正，邊進步邊認識。盧師常對王老師講：不要講過去那般的好，過去再好那是過去，這般就不靈了，你們識字（呀），要去撈啊，咱這拳深入海底。

王老師也多次重複盧師的話給我們聽：學拳不要局限在過去，過去的好不能成為現在發展的桎梏，過去的好只能是現在學習的營養，繼承和發展是一片葉子的兩個面，要一起成長。

向盧老師學習，一是要繼承前輩們的創新成果。我去過盧師的家鄉訪過拳，前輩們講的最多的一句話就是：盧老師把拳改了，不一樣了。第一代傳人中的解興邦老師，在上世紀七十年代創造性地整理出一套打拳的方法，具有即時性、可操作性，極大程度地發揮了它的實用性，豐富了盧式心意，使這一時期在上海及長江中下游地區盧式心意空前的繁榮。

王書文老師在上世紀六十年代末便開始與盧師的大弟子李尊賢、楊肇基等諸多老師一道全面系統地整理盧式心意的理論、動作盤法、用法和教學。2005 年10 月1 日與盧師之子盧少君老師及其他同門共同發起成立了盧式心意六合拳研究會，為的是更加系統地研究、整理、學習盧師留給我們的遺產。

繼承本是與前輩們接上氣，通上話，有了香火的延續，繼承的是前輩們不囿成見的創新。很是幸運，前輩們的部分創新成果因為有我們的繼承得以保存延續，成為了現在的血脈之本。

向盧老師學習，二是要繼承前輩們的創新精神。因為有了前輩們的努力、創新，盧式心意在上海，在全國的武術界有了影響，贏得許多人的關心、尊重，有了許多溢美之詞，使它得以流傳、發展。但不要因為練的人多了，有了嬌情，有了固執，少了相容，把盧師及前輩們留下的創新成果寵為新的不可逾越的新規成見，而忘了「心意」二字的含意。

一心一意地由衷打拳，多是個人的感受與感悟，沒有對與錯。在入形階段，只有符合不符合拳理，符合不符合因人而異、因材施教的傳統。在入相階段，只有喜歡與不喜歡之說。到了入定的階段，更是不用理會他人的喜歡與否，只要自己喜歡，就行了。

　　向盧師學習，打拳要經心、用心，隨時隨地在狀態中。

4. The Legacy of Master Lu

Master Lu has left us for almost 50 years, but there is nobody in Shanghai who has yet surpassed him in terms of moral character and martial art skill. I often hear that others tell his stories both inside and outside the martial art circles, and I also often tell others his stories as if Mr. Lu were still living among us and we could still hear him talk and see him practice.

Mr. Lu lived a life full of hardships. He was poor and illiterate, only capable of writing his own name. The only thing he did whole-heartedly was practice martial arts. Although he was not the first nor the last Wushu teacher in Shanghai, he was the one who created a martial art of his own style in Shanghai and became a grand master of his generation. He earned his fame and retired after a successful career in Shanghai.

Mr. Lu was diligent in practicing martial arts. He liked to think and practice. He had no prejudice against other martial schools and was good at communicating with them and adopting their merits. He was not conservative but inherited the essence of traditional martial art with creativity. He studied and practiced, pondered and improved, making progress on the technique and deepening the understanding of theory.

Mr. Lu said once to Mr. Wang, "Do not always talk about how good the past was. The past is in the past anyway and no longer of any use. You are all literate, so go reach into the sea of knowledge." Those words were repeated to us by Mr. Wang many times. Do not let martial art skills be limited by the past. Do not let the merits of the past shackle development; instead, let them become its nourishment. Inheriting and developing are like one sides of a leaf, both growing at the same time.

Today as we learn from Mr. Lu, first we inherit his creative achievements. I have visited Mr. Lu's hometown once. Seniors there told us that Mr. Lu had changed the techniques. Xingbang Xie, a second generation disciple of Lu Style Xinyi Quan, created an instantaneous and exercisable method in the 1970s which made the martial art easier to practice. It enriched the Lu Style Xinyi and brought unprecedented prosperity to the art of the period in Shanghai and the Yangtze River area.

In the 1960s, cooperating with Mr. Lu's senior disciples Mr. Zhunxian Li, Mr. Zhaoji Yang, and other teachers, Mr. Wang began to comprehensively and systematically compile the theory, techniques, application and teaching methods of Lu Style Xinyi. On October 1, 2005, Mr. Shaojun Lu(the son of Master Lu) and his fellow disciples established the Lu-style Xinyi Liu He Quan Club for systematic research, organizing and study of the legacy that Mr. Lu left to us.

To inherit means to communicate with our predecessor not only by learning from them the basic theories and techniques on martial art but also by developing the theories and techniques. It is fortunate that their tradition and creation have been passed down to us, becoming the foundation for the present.

So, in studying Master Lu, we should also inherit our predecessors's pirit of innovation. It was thanks to their efforts that Lu Style Xinyi has become influential nationwide, gaining care, respect, and praise from people, and has become spread and developed. When the number of people who practice Xinyi has increased so, we must remind ourselves not to be self-content, dogmatic and less accommodating.

The creative achievements of Mr. Lu and other predecessors should not become new limits. We must always remember the true meaning of "Xin Yi" (the heart and the mind). Xinyi Quan puts individual feeling and comprehension first and emphasizes using one's heart and mind in practicing rather than making distinction between right or wrong. At Ru Xing (learning the appearance of the movements), the basic principle and the tradition of giving different instruction to different people should be followed; at the stage for deepening the understanding (Ru Xiang), it is only the perception of liking or not; at the stage of having mastered the technique both in mind and action (Ru Ding), there's even less need to worry about what others think; it's enough if you enjoy it.

We should follow the example of Mr. Lu to practice Xinyi Quan through heart and with heart, and keep this in our spirit anytime and anywhere.

盧式心意・入形
Lu Style Xinyi-Imitating

一、單操多盤

盧式心意打拳繼承並延續了單兵相持的訓練方法，以單操多盤為法，有活步、定步兩種形式。單操，可以顧名思義地講是單個操練，具有強化性、快速上手性。

拳打千萬遍，強化了拳架的規整、軌跡的合理性，使習者有了深度記憶，就能形成條件反射，可以養成在無意識的情況下對外部環境做出及時正確的反應。如同現代軍事中的拼刺刀，幾個動作，一個士兵在他入伍期間，不斷地練習，千百次、千萬次地重複，不斷地加深記憶，熟能生巧，不怕會千招，只怕一招毒。短兵相接，分外眼紅，下意識地選擇撥與刺，你就能贏得生命。

能在一思前，莫在一思後。在單操的過程中可以解決拳術中的任何問題。

打拳的速度初時可以打得緩一些，要邊打拳、邊想拳、邊感覺、邊糾正，保持打拳的速度、心中感受的速度、思考改正的速度三位一體，給感受留有餘地，給修正留有空間。寧可打得慢一點，打一個接近對的拳，而不要打十個離正確愈來愈遠的拳。

單操多盤，因為只想一把拳，只有一把拳的週而復始，沒有多餘的連接、累贅分心。要做到拳拳見心，拳拳有感覺，拳拳有的放矢，有心而發。可以尋著一點點的感覺反覆地打、顛倒顛地打、耐心地打、不惜功夫地打，爾後是豁然開朗，以一貫十。

1. Repeat Single Movement

The Lu Style "Xinyi Quan" adopts and continues the single training method, which concentrates on practicing single movements. It can be practiced with the Moving Step or Staying Step method. This method is used to train people to have fast reactions. After repeating an action thousands of times, the postures and movements will become more natural and accurate.

It also deepens one's memory and helps one to develop conditioned reflexes, making one's movements instinctive, and able to respond correctly with precise timing in various environments. The military uses the same techniques to train soldiers to use the bayonet. When a soldier practices the same movement thousands and thousands of times, his memory has been deepened and his skill will be perfected.

A proverb says: "mastering one skill is more useful than knowing thousands of them." When two soldiers face each other in the field of battle, there is no time to think and only the one who automatically takes the right action will survive. Take an action before thinking. Repeating a single movement can solve many problems which met during the training.

At the beginning of training, move slightly slower, making an effort to think about the movement and to correct errors as they occur. Keep the movement's speed at a certain level where you can recognize and correct errors in order to improve your skill. Making one slow movement is much better than making ten of them with errors.

Repeating the same movement many times helps one to focus on a single thing without being distracted from the real goal. Make sure every movement comes from the heart and is aimed at a target, then hold it and repeat it patiently. When you know the true meaning of it, you can understand and master the skill easily.

二、打拳由衷見心

和別的門派功夫比較，盧式心意本身是象形取意的拳種，天生具有趣味性。心意二字可以天馬行空般地想像，一如國畫中的寫意、大寫意，書法中的草書、狂草一樣，要有所感、有所悟，才能有所行。打拳一定要由衷見心。

前人的經驗很重要，盧式心意在用的層面上說是一門技術，是技術就有投機取巧的方法和有事半功倍的竅門，這些法子、竅門其實是前輩們的認識、心血和智慧。

學習盧式心意，先要登上這條船、騎上這匹馬，帶上這枷鎖，這船、馬、枷鎖就是盧式心意前人留下來的技術。你若不上船、上馬、戴上枷鎖，只有一個方法，從頭再來過，再發明一次鑽木取火。

要虛心聆聽前人的智慧，用心感受前人的技術，與前人接上氣，通上話，戴上他的枷鎖在心上，打上他的烙印在身上，有了規矩心就不再是無依無靠，就算踩上了西瓜皮也劃不到哪裡去，心的自由一定是在意的方圓之中。熟能生巧之後總結自己的心得，感悟自己的技術，跟著感覺走，你是什麼樣的人，就能練出什麼樣的盧式心意六合拳來。

學習盧式心意拳打開頭就不要為技術而技術，做了技術的奴隸，被技術化了。

一是要有的放矢，要有敵情觀念，帶著敵情來打拳。習練時，前若有人驚之、應之。打拳就是演習預案，獲得執行預案的能力，道理在於學會帶著敵情學習預案、演習預案，危急時刻，下意識地選擇預案並執行預案。

二是要用心打拳，用心感受。學武之人要執著，使技術有了你的精神，你才能打拳開心一輩子。回首看，拳史上凡能開宗立派的大師，都是把技術個人化、人文化，使它們有了人的烙印。他的包融性越大，立派就越長遠；個性化越強，特點就越清晰。大師之所以成為大師，就是他隨手拈來的都是有生命、有人文精神的，可以用心感受到是有人氣的東西。

三是要有趣味地打拳，而不是被動地認真學習。不高興了，不練了，就一股腦地全還給了老師，好像給老師打拳似的，自己一點都不剩。所以打拳一定是自己有興趣，有主觀能動性，就是練一段時間停了、不練了，你自己還會給自己剩一點。

打拳最怕的就是把拳給打油了，無心慣了，兩兵相持時，就死定了。

2. Practicing from a Sincere Heart

Compared to other Martial Art styles, Lu Style "Xinyi" gains spirit by imitating the movements of animals. It is interesting. The words of Xin Yi, can be imagined, as the freehand brushwork in traditional Chinese painting: Big Freehand Brushwork, Cursive Hand, or Wild Cursive Hand in the Chinese calligraphy. You must practice with true feelings and understanding and have a sincere heart.

Our predecessors' experiences are very important. Lu Style "Xinyi" has useful techniques. It has its own approaches and tricks that came from the knowledge, efforts , and wisdom of our predecessors.

These experiences are like boats, horses, and chains. Learn the techniques of Xinyi as if you are boarding the boats, riding the horses, and taking the chains. If you are not on board, you have to start all over again and begin at the beginning. To avoid wasting time, open your mind and listen to the wisdom of our predecessors, feel the techniques of our predecessors, make a connection and communication with our predecessors, and put the chains on one's heart. Mark their marks on your body. Once you know the rules, your heart has a goal. Even if your feet are on a shell of a watermelon, your body would not fall, since the freedom of the heart is in the scope of the mind. Practice therefore makes it perfect. Then summarize your own experiences; sense your own technique; follow your own instincts. The level of Xinyi achieved depends on what kind of person you are.

First, one should not learn the techniques mechanically; otherwise, you will become a slave of the techniques. Instead, first, like shooting an arrow, you should have a clear target as if you are facing an enemy. When practicing it, pretend there is someone in front of you and try to surprise him. The purpose of this training is to actually rehearse a plan and learn to unconsciously execute the plan at a critical moment.

Second, box with heart and feeling. A martial artist must be undeviating in practicing; putting your own spirit into the techniques, which, in turn, will make it fun. Looking back at the history of the martial arts, it is found that all great masters who created their own martial arts styles have imprinted their own personality and spirit into the skills. The more comprehensive the style, the more far-reaching it is; the more personalized the style, the more distinctive it is. The reason masters become masters is because, for every movement they made, even casually, it is full of life and culture that you can feel as if it is alive.

Third, learn Martial Art with active enjoyment, not just passively. If you are not happy, do not do it. Otherwise, if you only learn it for your teacher, you will not learn anything. Therefore, you must be self motivated; in this way, you will remember the skills long after you have stop practicing.

The worst thing is to practice superficially, which will result in no real learning and will lead to complete defeat in a fight.

三、比較中進步

打拳是件動手的事，是肢體語言，諸多個為什麼多滲透在打拳的過程中。一分汗水才能有一分感悟，一分收穫才能有一分的快樂。要多思考、多體悟、多比較，在比較中找到動作要領，在比較中找到動心之處。

比較初於模仿，學生模仿老師，天經地義，一條捷徑很正確，這叫入形。入形就要模仿得形似，糾正拳架，合順軌跡，與老師的比較中，十之八九像就行，不可能是一模一樣，因彼此身形不同，此一時彼一時的環境也不相同。

比較時要有所思悟，動腦子。打拳最喜的就是有感覺，天分高的與常思考的，方法對路子，就會常有感悟；反之則少。

入形，是手把手的教，用眼睛看，照著來，要形似。如書法中的描紅、臨摹，是兩個實體間的比較。

入相，比較的是留在腦子中的一個印象、一個勢樣，虛的，要的是神似。如書法中的背帖。

入定，定能生慧，則是另一番景象，心有所思，意有所動，手有所成，要的是一個勢。一如水之漫延，求勢不求形，用意不用力，隨圓就方，比較的是人的趣味趨向和精神意味。

盧式心意是一門短拳，講究的是打人不露形，露形不為能，動作幅度不大，所以只有在用心觀察中、細心比較中、全神貫注地感覺中才能找到，若如此，拳才能打得有模有樣有精神。不比不知道，一比嚇一跳。打拳的快樂源於進步，今日與昨日不同，感覺到了昨日不曾有過的變化、昨日不曾知道的道理。不怕千招會，只怕一招精，單一把拳的比較要有時間的延續性，與昨天比、前天比、上週比和與第一印象比，感覺會更踏實、幸福和快樂。

3. Making Progress with Comparison

Boxing is a matter of acting and also a language of the body and limbs. It presents many "Whys" in the process. However, hard work is its own reward. Think more, experience more, and compare more. Find the essential truth to what you are learning and compare it to previously learned skills.

Comparison begins with imitation. It is right and proper for students to imitate their teachers. One begins by imitating the appearance first. This method is called "Ru Xing" (Imitating at Beginning) and is an effective approach. Also, try to correct errors by accurately tracing the movements of the teacher. It is enough to be 80–90% accurate. It is impossible to be 100% accurate because of differences in body shape and environment.

When you compare your movements with the teacher's, replay your movements over in your mind and feel the differences.

At this stage of Ru Xiang, one will be trained step by step. In the same way we learn to write with a brush, watch the teachers' movements and try to mimic them constantly comparing your own movements with the teachers.

At the "Ru Xiang" stage, compare the mental image of the perfect movement with your actual movements as if tracing a character in calligraphy.

Quietly meditate in a standing or sitting position making your self bright and lead yourself to a different mental landscape. In this place, one's mind, heart, and actions become one. The powerful forces around you are not defined by the objects placed before them, but rather, flow just as water pervades without caring

about shape or form. Use the mind to follow a circle or a square as needed. What are being compared are one's favorite movements and their spirit.

Lu Style Xinyi is mainly employed for short range fighting. Fight without exposing your intention. Exposing your intention means you are not capable yet. Therefore, all the movements are small. Only when you observe and feel with heart, carefully comparing, you can make it elegant and spirited. If you do not compare with others, you will never know. You will be surprised by the comparison. The enjoyment of learning comes from feeling the progress that you have made, from the differences between today and yesterday, from the changes that you never had before, from the principles that you never knew before. Mastering one is much better than knowing thousands. By comparing with yesterday, the day before yesterday, last week, and the first day, you will have more confidence and enjoyment.

四、拳架、軌跡、精神

打拳首先要的是拳架的規整，因為他關乎著你的武術壽命。拳架就像現代建築中的框架，關乎著能否矗立久遠，架構的合理是要所有重量都穩穩地落在地基上，不能落到架構中某一點上，否則樓必塌。

拳也如此，盧式心意的拳架要求人體所有重量，都要穩穩落到腳下的地上，所有發力都要源於腳下的地上，不能落在人體的某一點上，也不能撐在人體的某一點上，否則必痛。

打拳應從拳架的規整入手，糾正拳架的過程其實也就是抻筋、拔骨、長肌的過程，一定要跟著感覺走，要一點點地感覺，一點點地找，一點點地糾正。要領有二：一是保持肩膀與脊柱骨的正確關係；二是保持拳架中垂直線的垂直，並與其他線關係的正確。

肩膀與中軸的關係是一個三角形，是不倒翁的架構，頭欲上，肩欲沉，肘欲垂，脊椎欲挺。肩愈沉、肘愈垂，中軸就必須愈加挺拔、愈加上頂、愈加上領，人才能愈穩，才能做到不前傾，不後倒，不左斜，不右歪，有掤藝。人能直立行走是肩膀與中軸正確關係的作用。

盧式心意只有兩個基本的拳架：夾剪之式與牟杆之式。要理解這兩個拳架，就必須瞭解他們的架構。

夾剪之式：有三條垂直線：中軸線（脊椎）的垂直、前腿小腿的垂直、後腿大腿的垂直。有了這三條垂線的垂直，就能做到人體所有的重量都能穩穩地落於地上。

牟杆之式：禦敵之前的沾實一點與後腿保持直線，腳撐在地上，如一根頂門杆插在地下、頂在門後，發力於根，前腿小腿垂直地面。有這一條頂直的直線，就能做到消息全憑後腿蹬，發力於腳下。

彎彎套、環環扣、疊疊生是盧式心意技術的形象說，似彎非彎，似直非直，似正非正，要建立在垂直和頂直的基礎上。

軌跡。拳架的規整是運動軌跡合理的保證。盧式心意的運動軌跡是圓中求直。圓是守，守是有意識的；直是打，攻是下意識的，直是呈現在圓與圓之間，圈裡圈外求一點。拳譜曰：「陰陽二式在其間。」盧式心意是一門短拳，要的是貼身短打，圓中求直的軌跡是用一個「搓」字，如揉面搓泥、和線搓繩……力走「S」形或「8」字形。

搓就是擠開脂肪把力點進去。雙把要暗合一勢，同操一式，同時完成一個動作。運動中雙把有高低、上下、左右之分，呈現的形態不同，但內裡是一式，如持槍的雙手。拳譜曰：「戴九履一左三右七二四為肩六八為足」，是盧式心意身法的數字定位。

軌跡須嚴格按要求相合，其訣竅為：身體無論是定式或在運動中，軌跡亦無論是左右或右左、上下或下上、左上右下或左下右上，通過中心相加為十五，亦是折中節、塌中節、擰中節。上下束一，手過怕拿法，腳過怕跌法，缺則被人打，多則老，少則欠，不傷人，只會自傷和招人打。三三為九，三翻九轉為一體。若明此理，若如此行，外三合自合，身形自中

	離九 Li 9	
巽四 Xun 4		坤二 Kun 2
震三 Zhen 3	中五 Zhong 5	兌七 Dui 7
	坎一 Kan 1	
艮八 Gen 8		乾六 Qian 6

正，拳勢自和順，是打拳時運動軌跡的不二之法門。

拳的精神是建立在拳架規整、運動軌跡合理的基礎上，拳有精神，而打拳的人才能愈發有精神，才能有一股勁在內心裡鼓蕩，血氣充盈，左右輾轉不停勢；拳勢引導你，你才能不翼而動，才能因勢利導、依律而行，既而有了勝利之氣，有了靈性，人才會更有精神。依律一是控制，二是節奏。

4. The Quan Frame, Moving Path and Spirit

It is very important to have a standardized Quan frame, since it concerns your Wushu life. Like the framework in a modern architecture, how long that the building will last is of concern. Good architecture puts the weight firmly onto the foundation, not onto a certain point, otherwise the building will collapse. So does the Quan frame, which also needs to put the entire weight of your body firmly onto the ground under your feet. All the force should come from the ground, not from some points of your body or to some points of your body. Otherwise you might get hurt.

Therefore, start with a standardized boxing frame, which can be reached by stretching the tendons, pulling the bones, and growing the muscles. You have to follow your sensibility and know the movements gradually. Find errors and correct them one by one. There are two points: first to maintain "Bear Shoulders" in the right position with the spine; second to maintain the center line of the frame vertically and keep a right position with other parts of your body.

Bear Shoulders and the central line of the body form a tri-angle shape, which is a stable structure. Hold up the head; sink the shoulders; drop the elbows, and erect the spine. Sink the shoulders and elbows to keep the central line stretched, upright, and the body stable. Do not lean forward or backward, or left, or right. The proper position of the shoulders and the central line cause human beings to walk upright.

There are only two basic boxing frames in Lu Style Xinyi: the Clip and Cut (Jia Jian Shi), and the Prop the Pole (Dai Gan Shi) postures.

To understand these two frames, you must learn their

structures. In the Clip and Cut posture, there are three vertical lines: the central axle line (the spine), the lower calf of the front leg, and the thigh of the rear leg. Only when these three lines are kept upright can the entire weight of the body be firmly onto the ground.

In Prop the Pole posture, prepare to face an opponent, keeping the back leg straight, the ball of the foot on the ground, which supports the body like a pole into the ground and behind the door. The force comes from the foot. The lower calf of the front leg is perpendicular to the ground. By pushing the back leg against the ground, the force is generated form the bottom of the foot. Curves residing in curves, rings residing in rings, and layers upon layers are used to describe the techniques of Lu Style Xinyi. It seems bending but not really, seemingly straight but not, seemingly upright but not either, all of it built on vertical and straight support.

Moving Path is based on the standardized frames. In Lu Style Xinyi, it means to make a straight line in a circle. The circle means defense, which is conscious; the straight line means attack, which is subconscious. The straight lines reside between the circles. Try to find a point to strike in the circles. The verses said: "Yin and Yang intertwine in circles." Lu Style Xinyi is short range combat, striking closely. The movement of

盧式心意六合拳開拳

"to make a straight line in a circle" can be achieved by rolling and twisting, as if kneading dough or twining a rope. The force goes along to trace the shape of an "S" or an "8".

Twisting (Cuo) is to squeeze the flesh away and strike to the inside. Both hands should unite as one and act simultaneously. Both hands might not be at the same level; one might higher than another; or one might be upward and one downward; or one might be at the left and one at the right. Though they are at different positions, they are serving the same purpose, as if holding a gun with both hands. The boxing theory has developed a formula to describe the movement. It divides the body into nine parts and defines them with nine numbers (See the picture below): "Li 9" represents the head; "Kan 1" represents the feet, "Zhen 3" represents the left hand, "Dui 7" represents the right hand, "Kun 2" represents the right shoulder; "Xun 4" represents the left shoulder; "Qian 6" represents the right foot; "Gen 8" represents the left foot.

Their positions and movements must strictly follow the rules: no matter if the path is from left to right or reverse; or from higher to lower or reverse; or from the upper left to the lower right or reverse, the sum of the number on the path is fifteen, which also is known as Bend the Middle Part (Zhe Zhong Jie), Sink the Middle Part (Ta Zhong Jie), and Wring the Middle

Part (Ning Zhong Jie). Unify the upper and lower body as one. If the hands reach too far, one will be seized; if the feet reach too far, one will fall down. Or if they do not reach far enough, one will be beaten or will hurt himself. 3 rows x 3 columns are 9, no matter if they are the 3 turns or 9 transformations, they are all one unit. If one understands the rules and follows them, his three external harmonies will be unified automatically, his body will be centered and stable, his movements will be coordinated, which are the unique rules for 'Moving Path'.

The spirit of a martial art is based on standardized frames and reasonable moving paths. When the movements are full of energy, the boxer gains more spirit and power to arouse the Qi and blood inside.

Only when you let the movements lead you and you follow the rules, you will have vigor and a victorious spirit. To follow the rules means to control your body, and also the speed and the rate of the movements.

五、四梢齊

梢是末端的意思，四梢是指人體四大機體的最末端。四大機體是肉、筋、骨、氣血。舌為肉梢，牙為骨梢，甲為筋梢，髮為血梢，拳譜曰：「四梢齊，則可變其常態，能使人生畏懼焉。」齊是指一個物體上下束一、無先無後的一塊擱在那，既不頂也不丟。

四梢齊是說人體渾圓一體的狀態，上下束一，一個整體。沾著梢節亦如動中節、根節，沾著根節亦如動中節、梢節，一枝動百枝搖。但梢之內不是一成不變，而是自有變化，因為人是有內心嚮往的高級動物，因為意不同，時間久了而呈現出來的形態也不相同，或大了或小了、或軟了或硬了……

四梢齊是有意的，而梢之內裡齊是因為四梢節齊才齊的，是無意識的，所以又有人才誤為是鬆。四梢齊之法：髮欲衝冠（豎），牙欲斷金（咬），舌欲摧齒（頂），甲欲透骨（扣）。

四梢齊之法終是要落在盧式心意門人的身上，否則你就入不了盧式心意的門。盧式心意的肌肉工作群用的是膨脹肌，講究的是硬膨力拔，往外擴張，以膨為主。筋的工作狀態是伸拔，骨的狀態體現在膜與關節處，一個「開」字。氣血的狀態是「湧」，哪裡沾實那裡就拍岸驚起，用整體之勁。

盧式心意把人分為三節，三三為九的含義之一是有一個開拔關節的方法。依次是從三節中的梢開始（肩），次而是梢之梢（手腕）與根之梢節（腳腕）和中之梢節（頸）開始，再而是中節、根節，外用撐、拔、擰、拉……內裡多用一個「撬」字，槓桿原理，在後面支一個東西，這個東西可有可無，靠自身的重量撬開這個關節。如開肩關節就是在腋下夾一個東西，靠手臂自身的重量沉肩垂肘來橇開肩關節。

盧式心意關節撐開後用一個「系」字，一根筋或一組筋，是活關節。除此之外，還須明白與之對應的九竅，打拳時內裡開橇，心裡開竅，外鬆筋骨皮，內順氣血於九節之內。

梢節之竅：肩井穴為梢之根竅，肘曲池穴為梢之中竅，勞宮穴為梢之梢竅。中節之竅：氣海為下丹田，為中之根竅；膻中為中丹田，為中之中竅；眉衝為上丹田，為中之梢竅。梢節之竅：胯環跳穴為根之根竅，膝陽陵穴為根之中竅，腳湧泉穴為根之梢竅。

上述都是人體整齊之法。打拳還得有見性、聽性、勇性。

5. Four Ends Unified

In Chinese, "Shao" means the ends. Four Ends means: the end of the muscles, the end of the tendons, the end of the bones, and the end of the blood in a human body, which are the tongue, the teeth, the nails, and the hairs in turn. A boxing verse says: "when the four ends are unified, your appearance could scare an enemy". "Unified" means that the entire body, from the top to the bottom, is tied to one, as one part, so are the four ends. When the ends move, the middle and root sections move as well and vice versa.

That is: "one branch moving, undreds of branches shaking". However, inside the ends, it is not static but changing. Because humans are beings with minds, the shapes may vary according to the mind, which could be larger or smaller, softer or harder, and so on.

The unification of the four ends can be achieved intentionally, but the unification of the inside of the ends is subconscious, therefore some people misunderstand it as 'relaxing'. The unifying methods are: Hairs Push up a Hat (Hairs stand up), Teeth Break Metal (Bite), Tongue Crushes Teeth (Press), and Nails Penetrate Bones (Dig).

Anyone who wants to master Lu Style Xinyi has to learn to unify the four ends. Lu Style Xinyi uses the technique of pulling, extending, and mainly swelling to exercise the muscles; Stretch tendons; Exercise the joints and membrane of the bone. The working state of the Qi and the blood is "surging"; no matter which part of the body touches an opponent, the Qi and blood will be stirred with an integrated energy.

Lu style Xinyi divides a human body into three parts (End Part, Middle Part, and Root Part), and each part is divided into three sections (End Section, Middle Section, and Root Section). One meaning of the formula $3 \times 3 = 9$ is one way to exercise the joints, that is: to exercise in turn the shoulder, the wrist, and the neck, then the Middle Part and Root Part. For the external, use Propping (Cheng), Pulling out (Ba), Wringing (Ning), and Dragging (La). For the internal, mainly use the weight itself to exercise the joints. For example, in order to exercise the shoulder's joints, put a thing under the armpit and sink the shoulder and the elbow. The joints become more flexible. Besides, there are nine key points corresponding to the nine sections. When practicing the Quan, the internal are opened, the heart opened; the tendons, bones, and skins are relaxed. The Qi and blood inside the nine sections are smoothed. There are 3 key points on an arm: Jian Jing Xue, an acupuncture point on the shoulder, which is the root; the Qu Chi Xue, an acupuncture point on the elbow, which is the middle; Lao Gong Xue, an acupuncture point on the hand, which is the end.

The key points on the middle part of the body are: the Qi Hai Xue, an acupuncture point on the lower Dan Tian; Shan Zhong Xue, an acupuncture point on the middle Dian Tian; Mei Chong Xue, an acupuncture point on the upper Dan Tian. The key points on the root part of the body are: Huan Tiao Xue, an acupuncture point on the hip, Yang Ling Xue, an acupuncture point on the knee, and the Yong Quan Xue, an acupuncture point on the foot.

All above is about the method to unify the entire body. Besides that, you must have courage and the abilities of observing and listening.

六、野　戰

盧式心意打拳要「留藝不留成」，留藝就是下一把不打你，不留成就是這一拳全力以赴地打。「龍之驚，虎之恨，狼之心」，獸心野性任意行，要有野心、野性、野勁、野意。對抗我們稱之為：野戰。

野戰開始時為亂戰，無章無法；久了，有了章法。章法是在野戰過程中積累出來的認識、心得和技術。章法開始的時候體現為糾正錯誤，過一段日子就少犯錯誤，最後是不犯錯誤。

野戰的魅力就是未知，人人都有慾望，面對已知，有安全、有享樂；面對未知，驚心動魄的感覺，全神貫注。入門（初級）學會用拳打，開拳（中級）要手腳並用，戴好護具，用入門時的無法、無知，去面對未知。

野戰開始時不要多想技術，要勇敢，豁得出去，看似不講究，生澀的打法卻彰顯出一個習武人的本色，蘊育著一個正確的選擇，一個有生命的內核。不要讓現成的技術、章法和所謂的成功經驗左右一個未知的生命，變得縮手縮腳，而是要真心感受，靠自己。在野戰的過程中尋找自我，而不是照樣複製，照本宣科。打拳一定要你是你，我是我，要有以我為主的心態，讓技術自然萌芽、成長。

相信這世上沒有一個完全相同的我，沒有一套現成的技術完全適合我。要認真面對每一個對手，經歷從無法逐漸到有法的過程。多少年後驀然回首，初入門時的經歷、經驗是最難得的，是突破技術瓶頸、回歸自我、登高望遠時的鑰匙。

每一次的面對未知，都要清空自己，以無知來面對未知，這樣精神貫注，狀態一心，態度認真，適應及時，提高也最快。技術在過程中生根發芽，認識在過程中提高。你要有縱向的比較，把野戰中的每一個小感受經常性地串起來認識；還要橫向比較，把單操的技術用進來，諸多個預案拿來實訓，在實踐中進步。

用無知、無法去面對未知，挨打是必然的。這次這樣被打，下次你就會這樣打別人，在挨打中成長了。

6. Ye Zhan（Wild Combating）

In Lu Style Xinyi Quan, there is a saying "save some tricks but not the power", which means to use all the power to fight. One should have "dragon's alertness, tiger's hatred, and a wolf's heart". With the heart of an animal, with wild nature, wild strength, and wild intention, fight like an animal. Therefore we call it Wild Combating (Ye Zhan).

There are no routines for you to follow at the beginning of the practice of Wild Combating. But after a while, you will gradually accumulate your own experience and have your own rules. By correcting the mistakes you made during the fight, you will make less and less mistakes, and at last no mistakes.

The fascination of Wild Combating is that you do not know what can happen. Everyone has a desire for something. Facing a known thing, one feels secure and pleasurable; facing an unknown thing, one would feel the heart-stirring and have to concentrate his attention completely on his work. First, at the primary stage, learn to fight with fists, and then, at the middle stage, hands and feet are used together. You have to wear the protective gear, because you do not know what can happen.

At the beginning of the fight, you do not have to think much about techniques. Just to be ready to take risks and have the bravery to do what you can. Even though it does not look elegant, but it still shows the true personality of a person who knows Martial Arts and contains a right choice of a real fighting life. Do not bind yourself by the ready-made skills, regulations, and so called successful experiences, but trust yourself and depend on yourself and find yourself, rather than copy others or books. When fighting, keep yourself calm, claim yourself, and try to lead the fight, then your skills would improve automatically. Believe that there is no body exactly the same as yours and no off-the-shelf technology fully fit for you. To treat seriously all the opponents and the fights, your techniques will be naturally cultivated and boosted. Years later, when you recall it, you will find what you have experienced at the beginning is a key that breaks the bottleneck of the fighting technique and help you to find yourself and lead you to a higher level.

Every time when you face an unknown, empty yourself. The one who knows nothing, does not fear. Concentrate your mind on the fight and take it seriously. Respond on time and improve fast. Along this process, your technique will be built and your understanding will be enhanced fast. Compare these experiences with those in the past. Adopt the techniques that you have learned in the single movement exercise. Use the strategies in an actual combat, which will help you to make progress in the practices. At the beginning, you might be beaten. If you are beaten this time, you know how to beat him by the same way next time and your skills will be improved gradually.

七、野戰從哪裡下手

從哪裡下手不過是個出手經驗和習慣的事，要分清你、我、他，適合就對，不能一概而論。各有各的出手法子，各有各的門道；笨人有笨辦法，聰明人有聰明的法子，不一而同，條條大路通羅馬，你認為好就行。

把自己零星的經驗、習慣串起來，貫通了它們之間的關係，就有了自己的下手法子。要認識自己，找自己的路子，別人是學不會的。

打拳從哪下手並不重要，重要的是是否敢於下手，一勇二膽三功夫，要夠狠。把心中多大的恨意一股腦地發洩出來，想都不要想，劈頭蓋臉地拳打腳踢。寧在一思前，莫在一思後。打慣了，想久了，什麼都有了，要技術有技術，要觀念有觀念，要理論有理論，所習的預案能隨意用之，那不就是要創新就有創新了嗎。

野戰，盧式心意要求手腳齊到方為真。腳起是去，去不空去，要拳打腳踢；腳落要踩，踩不空落，要腳踩拳打。拳分三節，內含三種接手方法，梢節沾、中節沾、根節沾。如梢節沾，用中節或根節去沾實；中節沾，用梢節或根節去沾實；根節沾，用梢節或中節去沾實。無一定論，誰概念化了，誰絕對化了，也就離老朽不遠了。十四極分兩邊，頭、肩、肘、手、胯、膝、足。兩邊共有十四個地方好用、好打人，沾哪用哪，隨意用之無不可。

頭打起意占胸膛，起而未起占中央，腳踏中門搶地位，就是神手也難防。

肩打一陰返一陽，兩手隻在洞中藏，左右全憑蓋世力，束展二字一命亡。

肘打去意占胸膛，起手好是虎撲羊，或在裏胯一旁走，後手只在肋下藏。

把打頭落起手襠，降龍伏虎霹靂閃，天地交合雲遮月，武藝相戰蔽日光。

胯打中節並相連，陰陽交合必自然，外胯好似魚打挺，裏胯搶步變勢難。

膝打密處人不明，好似猛虎出木籠，和身輾轉不停勢，左右明撥下絕情。

足打踩意不落空，消息全憑後足蹬，與人交勇無虛備，去意好似捲地風。

野戰說到天邊也是一動手的事、實踐的事，從你最感興趣的地方下手，如對方的臉，再小一點，對手的鼻子。跟著感覺走，找你最想打的地方和能打到的地方。

7. Start a Wild Combating

How do you start a combat? It is a matter of a habit and experience. Use your own experiences and habits and use them well. Find your own way that suits you most.

It is not important how to start a fight, but to be fearless. There are three things you need: courage, boldness, and skills. Do not think, but attack, as if there is a great hatred in heart. Beat with hands and feet; beat before thinking of it. When you practice enough and summarize enough, you will master the techniques, concepts, and theories. You will be able to apply your strategies and create new ones as needed.

The Wild Combating of Lu Style Xinyi needs to use hands and feet at the same time. Lift a foot to kick and never go for nothing, and punch at the same time; put a foot down to stamp and never go for nothing, and punch at the same time. If we see the body in three sections, the end, the middle, and the root, there are three ways to fight, which are with the end, with the middle, or with the root. For an example, if you fight with the end, force comes from the middle and the root; if you fight with the middle, force comes from the end and the root; if you fight with the root, force comes from the end and the middle. But these rules can be altered as needed. Do not treat them as doctrine. You have 14 parts that can be used for a fight, which are a head, 2 shoulders, 2 elbows, 2 hands, 2 hips, 2 knees, 2 feet, and buttocks.

Strike with the head. The head follows the feet. Step into the center and hold a good position; you can not be defended by a soul.

Strike with the shoulders. Roll over the shoulders to exchange Yin and Yang; hide the hands; strike left or right, which depends on a powerful strength; extend or withdraw to take his life.

Strike with the elbow. Aim at the opponent's chest with elbows; lift a hand as if a tiger leaping on a lamb; or wrap the hips and move sideways; hide the back hand under the ribs.

Strike with the hands and use the head as a hand as if beating a dragon or a tiger like lightning; or as if the clouds cover the moon, hands and head cover him from the sun.

Strike with the hips and the middle part of the body, combining Yin and Yang naturally. Turn the hips as if a fish jumping; wrap around the hips and rushingly step to leave him no room.

Strike with the knees before he notices it, as if a fierce tiger escaping from the cage. Turn the body and continue to strike to the left or to the right.

Strike with the feet-stomping. The force is generated from

盧式心意六合拳開拳

the other foot pushing the ground. Always be ready for a fight, as if a wind sweeping the ground.

Wild Combating is no more than an action. Start from the place where you are interested in most, such as his face, or even smaller one–his nose. Follow your feelings and strike with your elbow, hand, or whatever. Target the part that you want to attack most and you are able to reach.

八、野戰遊戲

盧師常講：試把、試把。就是對抗一下，相互打一打。一般地點多在老師的家中。教拳的場所中，人員相互熟悉，多為同門或師兄弟。雙方各站一方，稱為本方區。有人講開始，雙方各前進1步或3步，視場地情況，然後在中間區開始對抗，稱為：交戰區。

多數情況下在五步之內，場地有正方形（約4m×4m），有窄長形（約2m×6m），有長方形（約4m×6m）。方法很簡單，誰先倒地誰輸，誰先出圈誰輸，僵持在哪一方哪方輸。

稍微嚴格一點的有老師或長者多說一句：「慢一點，點到為止。」在桌上敲兩聲，敲出一個節奏來，就像古代的擊鼓前進，鳴金收兵一樣。

規則（根據要求不同設計）。

盧式心意・入形

8. Competition on Wild Combating

Master Lu said often: To practice the fight means to let two people go against each other or to fight each other. The rules can be altered as needed. Players, who are usually fellows, are familiar with each other. Each of the players takes a site, which is called a Local Area. When a competition is started, both players take 1 or 3 steps forward according to the size of the room.

Then, start the competition in the center area, which is called Combating Area. In most cases, it is a square area (4m × 4m), or a rectangular area (2m × 6m or 4m × 6m). The one who first falls loses; the one who first moves out from the combating area loses; the one who fights at his Local Area and keeps a stalemate loses.

Teachers or elders sometime would remind the players to be careful and knock the desk to stop the competition, as if the ancient armies beating drums or gongs to withdraw their troops.

Competition Rules (altered as needed)

盧式心意・入相

Lu Style Xinyi・Into the Picture（Ru Xiang）

盧式心意六合拳開拳

一、關於心

秦時明月漢時關，萬里長征人未還。
但使龍城飛將在，不教胡馬度陰山。

　　每說心意時，就不由得想起漢時飛將軍李廣一事，「廣出獵，見草中石，以為虎而射之，中石沒鏃，視之，石也。因複更射之，終不能複入石矣……余嘗以問楊子雲。子雲曰：至誠則金石為開……」何也？一心一意。

　　心在內，內心的堅定似山；意在周，外意的驚靈似水。內心的勇敢、堅持、浩然，不是單純靠習武之術就能修來，須在日常的生活中養成。匹夫之勇，愚者無畏，算不得真正的勇敢。

　　相傳心意拳為民族英雄岳飛所創，用於殺敵報國。千百年來武穆精神流傳在代代心意門人的心中，愛國、感恩、正氣、大義、誠信，就是心意門人勇敢之心的本源。

　　國家有難，匹夫有責，大革命時期，堅持在白色恐怖地區的就有多位元盧式心意的門人，如盧師的大弟子李尊賢、解興邦……有了內心的勇敢，一顆心才會有堅持，才會有內心的堅定似山，才會有心安理得、從容鎮定，才會有信念。「行天下之道，得志與民由之，不得志獨行其道，有了富貴不能淫、貧賤不能移、威武不能屈的浩然之氣。」

天地間人是最有心嚮往的動物，有了內心的嚮往，才能主動地看到東西，才會有真心的喜歡。愛的一定是你內心嚮往的，不嚮往的東西就是放在你的眼前，也是視而不見。

我有一位寫書法的朋友，無論是寫大字或是蠅頭小楷，皆能閉上眼睛寫，一切了然於胸，什麼規矩呀、章法呀、已不成為規矩、章法，有的只是內心的那一點嚮往，動心之處，放大他，堅定他，使之成為主觀認定。

1. About the Heart

The Qin's moon still shines; and the Han's gates still stand,

But the soldiers from those battles have yet to return.

As long as heroes Qin Wei and Guang Li stand guard,

Hu's troop cannot pass Yin Mountain.

Once Xin Yi (Heart and Mind) is mentioned, I can not help but think of the story of Han Dynasty's General Guang Li: Once, Guang Li went to hunt. He saw a boulder in the grass and shot it with an arrow, thinking it was a tiger. The arrowhead was buried deep in the stone. Guang Li approached the boulder and found that it was not a tiger but stone. He shot the stone many more times, but it could take the arrowheads. When Mr. Ziyun Yang was asked for the reason, Ziyun said, "The utmost sincerity can influence even metal and stone." Why? Unify one's heart and mind as one.

The heart is within, and the internal heart could be solid like a mountain. The mind is outside, and the external mind could startle a soul like turbulent water. The bravery, determination, and noble spirit inside rely on martial arts and daily refining. An ordinary man's bravery and a fool's audacity are not real courage. According to the legend, Xinyi Quan was created by the national hero Fei Yue (Yue Wu Mu).

He used it to fight enemies to serve the country. For thousands of years, Wu Mu's spirit has been spread from heart to heart, from generation to generation in Yinyi schools. Patriotism, gratitude, principle, righteousness, and integrity are the sources of the brave hearts of Xinyi's disciples.

When the country is in trouble, everyone has responsibility to help. During the war, many famous disciples of Master Lu, such as Mr. Zunxian Li and Mr. Xingbang Xie were working in the danger zones. Only internal bravery can solidify the heart into a mountain, having good conscience, complete self-assurance and, faith. That is: "go on a righteous path and share the achievements; if not successful, calm yourself. Those are neither riches nor honours can corrupt him; neither poverty nor lowly condition can make him swerve from principle; neither threats nor force can bend him."

Human hearts are filled with desire, which initiates the feelings of sincere love. Love is a desire from the heart. If you do not aspire to do something, you can not see it even if it were in front of you. I have a friend who can write with his eyes closed, no matter a lower case character or big calligraphy; it's all in his heart. All the rules and techniques become a desire in his heart. Imagine it, then enlarge it, solidify it and realize it.

二、關於意

　　意，內裡傳達心的想法，外裡感應三界之象，是內心嚮往的外在表現，是動心之處的放大，看不到，也摸不著，但感覺得到。是臆想吧？答曰：是觀想。

　　內心的嚮往需要一個載體來外在表現，即可視的、能實際操作的東西。人往往會選擇世上最符合自己內心嚮往的東西，去模仿他，學習他，久而久之、合二為一就是有了意。有人說，人是高等動物，為什麼還要去學動物？因為現代人遠離自然，紮堆人群中，人的本能在漸漸退化，模仿動物其實就是淨化現代人紛雜的思緒，回歸本能。

　　盧式心意選擇雞、鷂、燕、鷹、虎……這十種動物，見其形取其意，在雞的身上尋到勇敢和欺鬥；在馬的身上尋到奔騰與洶湧；在臆想龍的身上尋到了驚靈、抖擻……隨著功夫的不斷長進，動作的不斷合順，你便會明白「意」在拳中是多麼重要。

拳有意，不是說拳架規整、運動軌跡正確就有意，而是在規整與運動的過程中是多麼富有意味、變化，感受深刻。

> 雞有欺鬥之勇，鷂有側展之骹；
>
> 燕有取水之巧，鷹有捉拿之功；
>
> 龍有撅骨之法，虎有撲食之功；
>
> 馬有奔騰之功，熊有掀鼎之力；
>
> 蛇有拔草之力，猴有縱身之靈。

意，在你忙碌的時候誰也想不起誰，只有在你閑下來的時候彼此才動了念頭。它躲在忙碌生活的後面，藏在抓時間促生產的後面，也躲在規矩、大聲吆喝的後面，你越是頭頭是道、振振有詞，意就會離你越遠一點。

它不是技術，不是熟能生巧就能得來的；不要有能打、能練就是有意的錯誤念頭。你看不到也摸不著它，但你有了一份好心情，從容而淡定、無慾而無求、心安而理得後，意才會悄悄地來到你身邊。

古人講：「窮文富武」，是說文與武的特性，現在還是這樣，富武，不是說你有多少錢，而是指你的好心情、好心態，你也可以像孔夫子的弟子顏回一樣，居窮陋而自樂，但多數情況下是飽暖後才能識得意。要有不為來錢，不為爭第一，不為養家糊口，不為生活而打拳的心態，要有超越行業習氣、匠氣的底蘊。

意的遺傳性源源深長，一門好武藝意經了你的手，你的基因就會留傳下去，這一門的人就會世世代代的記得你，就像我們現在記得岳飛、姬龍峰、買壯圖、盧嵩高……諸多前輩們一樣。

2. About the Mind （Yi）

Mind （Yi）, the connection between the inside and the outside. It is the outer manifestation of inner longing. It is the point of the heart, a feeling that is enlarged. You can not see it and touch it, but you can feel it. Is it imaginary? The answer: it is imaginary.

The inner longing needs to be expressed externally, to be seen and realized. People tend to choose the most desirable thing to represent their own inner world, imitating it and learning from it. Gradually, both unify as one, and Yi is working. Someone said human beings are clever than animals. So why do we learn from animals? Because the modern people are far away from nature and

盧式心意六合拳開拳

the human instinct is being degraded day by day. Imitating animals is actually cleaning confused thoughts of the modern people, allowing them return to their instincts.

Lu-style Xinyi chooses chicken, harrier, swallow, eagle, tiger etc., and total 10 animals. Imitate their behavior and take their purpose. From the chicken, we learn their braveness and indomitable will. From the horse, we learn their galloping and surging. From the imaginary dragon, we learn their spirit. With continuous effort, you will make constant progress in the movements and you will understand the importance of the "meaning" (Yi) in Xinyi Quan.

When we mention that there is Yi in Quan, it does not only mean the right structure and movements, but also the deep feelings of the structures and movements.

The chicken has the courage to fight. The harrier has the ability to fly sideways.

The swallow has the cunning to obtain water. The eagle has the power to hunt.

The dragon has a way to move their own bones. The tigers have the power to attack.

The horse has the skill to gallop. The bear has the strength to lift.

The snake has the sinew to pull up the grass. The monkey

has the agility to jump.

If you are busy with something else, you can not have Mind (Yi). Only when you have nothing to do and you start to think will you obtain it. It is hidden behind a busy life, behind the race to be productive, and behind the rules. The more clear and logical, you are, the more you will be away from Mind (Yi). It does not come from technology or perfected practice. Do not misunderstand that fighting or training can bring Mind (Yi). You can neither see it nor touch it, but when you're in a good mood, with no desire and demand, calm and peaceful, Mind (Yi) will come to you quietly.

An old saying said: "Poor Wen, Rich Wu". "Wen" means reading and writing; "Wu" means martial arts. This is the same today. "Rich Wu" does not mean to say how much money you have, but a wealth in spirit and character. You can be poor as the disciple of Confucius, Yan Hui, but happy. When you feel warm and satisfied, you will understand Yi. If you have no worry about money, no worry to be the best, no worry to feed your family, not for living to box, then you start to have Yi. You must go beyond the artificiality.

The heredity of Yi is long and deep. If a good martial art pass through you, your legend will remain and the disciples will remember you from generation to generation, as we remember the predecessors: Fei Yue, Long Feng Ji, Zhuangtu Mai, Songgao Lu and so on.

三、意的驚靈

靈動：陰陽間的變化，一形到另一形間的運動方法，一態到另一態間的變化方式。

靈是驚勁乍現，多顯於氣血表現。驚，用所謂四兩的勁，打破平衡，驚起體內氣血的晃動，帶動四梢的驚靈。驚靈，像閃電，疾不及閉目；驚，像驚雷，快不及掩耳；驚，像火，迅不及想……遇敵好似火燒身，寧在一思前，莫在一思後，就是一個「驚」字。

落實在身形上有曲斷中節，有恨天無把、恨地無環、反弓斷弦之意後，才能有一枝動而百枝搖，四梢驚而起，內勁驚而出。有了驚才成其了靈，有了六合才有了驚炸，身形上奔而出炸而開，才會有的是短、疾、快、利之藝。

驚靈是驚勁炸現、措手不及、出奇制勝。驚靈，先得心中有驚靈之應，腦中有驚靈之象，身體有感受。如大自然中的驚雷、閃電、虎撲、蛇咬……想要好，梢中求，多思四梢中的血梢。

形態上有動靜、緩疾、虛實、含野四藝，拳兒似水，時而平靜如初，時而奔騰咆哮，時而迂迴通幽，時而一瀉千里，時而慢若郎當，時而炫耀如電。

拳有虛實，去留有餘地，來留有空間；虛中有實，實中有虛；虛八九分實一二，實八九分虛一二；

盧式心意六合拳開拳

利於變化，如影隨形。飯，八分為飽，九分為撐，十分為脹，十二分要死人的。拳也一樣，虛之中沾實一點，把把沾實也是要累死的。

拳打含野。含，集中精力，一如懷中乳嬰，口中如玉，走若纖女，如十月懷胎，含著，緊不得，鬆不得，重不得，輕不得，含得住一口氣，沉得下一顆心。「慢若郎當龍掉膀」，側著重盤的就是這股含意。每一把拳中都有動靜、緩疾、虛實、含野四藝。野勁，男兒當自強，肆意橫行，這就不多講了，老輩們常講：打拳要野。

3. Yi（Mind） Startling the Soul

Ling(sprit or soul) Moving: When switching between Yin and Yang, switching from one movement to another, or switching from one posture to another.

Ling (sprit) is a startling force, which show the change of the blood and Qi (Internal Energy). "Startling" means using small force to break the balance and make the blood and Qi flowing quickly, and lead the sprit of the 4 ends (finger, tooth, hairs, and tongue) to startle a soul. "Startling the Soul" is like thunder, lightning, or a fire–it happens more quickly than you realize. When you meet an enemy, it's as if encountering a fire; you must act fast without having to think, which is an example of "startling".

The "startling" can be achieved by "Qu Duan Zhong Jie" (bending the middle part of your body), "Hen Tian Wu Ba" (hate the sky for not having a handle. if it had one, I could pull the sky down), "Hen Di Wu Huan" (Hate the earth for having no ring. If it had, I could lift the earth up) and the "Fan Gong Duan Xuan" (pull the bow backward to break the string). Shake one branch to move one hundred. Only when the 4 ends are startled and aroused, the interior strength bursts out. The "startled soul" makes Liu He (Six Harmonies) astonished and the body burst, which allows the boxing to be neat, fast, swift and sharp.

Startling the Soul is to render the opponent's defense inadequate and seize victory with an astonishing attack. To "startle", the heart has a reaction first. Then the brain has an image of "startling", and the body has a feeling of it. Feel it as if feeling the nature of thunder and lightning, a tiger pouncing, or a snake biting······ If you want to be good at it, feel and get it in the 4 ends, especially the end of blood.

There are four ways: Moving or Staying, Slow or Quick, Empty or Solid, Tame or Wild. Boxing is like water; sometimes it is calm, sometimes it gallops and roars, circuits quietly, rushes over hundreds of miles, wanders randomly, and sometimes it shows off like lightning. Boxing can be empty or solid, which leaves a space for moving or staying. The empty resides within the solid, the solid within the empty. When we say it is empty, it means that the empty is 8 to 9 of 10 and the solid is 1 to 2 of 10; when we say it is solid, it means that the solid is 8 to 9 of 10 and the empty is 1 to 2 of 10, which make the change more flexible, like a shadow following the figure. When we eat, to be 8 of 10 full is good; to be 9 of 10 is overfilled; 10 of 10 is bloated; and 12 of 10 could cause death.

It is the same in boxing. If it is solid all the time, you will be exhausted. "Hold" means to concentrate as if holding a baby in your arms, keeping a piece of jade in your mouth, or walking like a fine lady or a pregnant woman. Hold but not tightly, not loosely, not heavily, nor lightly. Hold a breath and calm the heart, slow as if a dragon swinging shoulders. Every movement includes the art of moving or staying, slow or quick, empty or solid, tame or wild. Wild force means that a man has to be strong all the time and fight wild. Some senior people said often: box wildly.

四、打拳入味

打拳對於多數人來說只是一個愛好；有癮了，戒不掉了，就是一嗜好。怎麼會有癮呢？因為打拳終究要的是敏感度，要你的筋骨皮比別人敏感，你的氣血比別人敏感，你的神經比別人敏感……聽風知雨，功夫越好的人越敏感，反應也越及時，感受也越是幸福，感覺也越是饑餓，一如背上的癢、心中的痕，愈抓愈癢，愈癢愈抓，因為你查得比過去細，知得比過去微，感得比過去深，幸福得比過去幸福，癢得比過去癢……心意如鉤，意氣繚人。

如何才能做得到呢？

答：兩點，一是刪繁就簡，二是臆想天開（入相）。

拳打到入相階段，要抓住動心之處，其餘皆可不顧。如搖閃把這一把拳，在入形階段，要盤五把藝，轉把、揚把、擰把、閃把、攢把，每一把都要盤得規整，要中規中距。

在入相階段你只需要盤三把意，或轉把、閃把、攢把；或揚把、閃把、攢把；或擰把、閃把、攢把。以閃把為中心，要的是「閃」字訣，甚至可以只盤閃把一把藝，其餘皆不盤。還說搖閃把這把拳，如何才能做到臆想天開？

細想，搖閃把為雞形，雞有欺鬥之勇，雞鬥時，雞的閃進之相要印入你的大腦中，有個視頻、有個圖像在腦海中，不斷地出現，不斷地模仿，不斷地合二為一，不斷地進步。「閃」字，你也可以模仿閃電、驚雷……有了觀想就有了意，天門就開了。

打拳就是喜歡，玩的是心中的嚮往，求的是隱藏在技術之後的東西，說的是打拳人的氣度、品格。日有所思，夜有所想，身有所悟，手有所現。想要入味，要全神貫注，物我兩忘，細緻入微，用心而發。味道只會生成於自然，不過分，不拘泥，不做作，自然有格。

4. Boxing with Feelings

Boxing is a hobby for most fans. Once you get into it, you can't give it up. Why would you get addicted to it? It is because the result of boxing is sensitivity; it will make your bones, skin, blood, and nerves more sensitive than those of others… Listening the wind and know the rain. The better Kung Fu you have, the more sensitive you become to people and the faster you can respond. The more happy you are, the more you want to learn, and like an itch on your back, the more you scratch, the more it itches; the more it itches, the more you scratch. Similarly the more detail you know, the deeper happiness you feel, the greater the itch becomes…… Xinyi (Mind) is like a hook, its Qi grabs hold of people.

How can you achieve the feelings? There are two way: one is to simplify it and the other is to picture it (Ru Xiang or Into a Picture）. Once you are in the stage of Ru Xiang, seize the heartbeat only and forget the rest. Using "Swinging and Dodging Hold" (Yao Shan Ba) as an example, in the first stage "Imitating", you have to practice Turning Hold (Zhuan Ba), Sinking Hold (Ta Ba), Wringing Hold (Ning Ba), Swinging Hold (Shan Ba) and Piercing Hold (Cuan Ba). All of them should be practiced according to the requirement and the standard. In the stage of "Into a Picture", you only need to practice three of them, either Turning Hold, Swinging Hold and Piercing Hold, or Sinking Hold, Swinging Hold and Piercing Hold, or Wringing Hold, Swinging Hold and Piercing Hold. Take "Swinging Hold" as a major feature. You can even only practice "Swinging and Dodging Hold" and nothing else at all.

Using "Swinging and Dodge Hold" as an example, how can you picture it?

"Swinging and Dodging Hold" came from the chicken form. When a chicken is fighting, its swinging and dodging imprints in your cerebrum and makes a picture in your mind. The picture appears constantly and you imitate it constantly. To unify them, you need constant progress. For the "dodging", you can imitate lightning, thunder······ Once you have the picture, you have Yi (mind) and the door to wisdom is opened.

Practice boxing because you like it. Practice it with a

yearning heart. Search for what hides behind the technology. Here we are talking about the characteristics of a boxer. Think at day time and dream at night time. When your body feels something, your hands show something. To feel boxing, you must concentrate on it, forget yourself and your surroundings, and feel every detail by heart. The feeling comes naturally, not overdone, constrained, or artificial, but natural within its standards.

五、盧式心意雙魚

　　盧式心意所有的技術動作都是在運動中完成，沾實一點也是在運動的過程中沾實，不是站定發力，我們稱為：活技。左右輾轉不停勢，寧要不是莫要停，行拳如水漫延，沾實如火燒身。整而言之，就是前進的過程中完成三翻九轉，驚靈如水、無常、快疾的源頭是胯與脊椎組合的運動。

　　消息全憑後腿蹬，關節曲折成形後的展開，像摺扇與開扇一樣，力沿著腳上升到膝、到胯。運動中的胯要調整出一個角度改變力的方向，以保持身體在運動中的中正。就像汽車極速奔馳在彎道上，彎道本身要有一個斜面，一邊厚一邊薄，這樣才會安全。我們常說要用胯走路、用胯打拳，這是本意。

　　轉動胯可以轉出不同個角度的圓來，不同的力沿著胯上升到腰脊椎骨，在三、四、五節腰脊椎骨處打了一個滾，細而言之就是以腰部的橫向肌肉運動帶動腰脊椎骨的三、四、五節轉動（腰傷的患者多傷於此。中而正、合而順，則不易受傷），帶動了體腔內氣血的變化，也使氣血有了目的地，力開始變化為勁。胯的角度愈大，腰脊椎骨滾動的力量愈大、速度愈疾，所產生的勁也愈強，沾實一點也愈深。

如果胯是水平轉動的，力在三、四、五節腰脊椎骨處打了一個滾，那麼力與勁的運動軌跡是「C」字形的；如果胯是有坡度的，力在三、四、五節腰脊椎骨處打了一個滾，那麼力與勁的運動軌跡是「S」字形或「8」字形的。

運動中轉胯形成的圓與脊椎骨的「S」線和力與勁的「S」線的組合便是盧式心意的雙魚圖，不同的一點，它是一個三維、立體、運動中變化著的雙魚圖。

外力來襲時，有意防守，主動防禦，外力由被沾實點傳到脊椎骨上，以脊椎骨為軸的左右擺動，逆來順受，直來橫掛；以胯有底盤的中節會上下晃動，逆來順受，橫來豎掛，盧式心意雙魚即可輕鬆化解。

外力來襲時，措手不及，被動防禦，外力由被沾實點傳到脊椎骨上，中軸線的「S」形會自動避讓，化解部分外力，剩餘的外力會沿著脊椎骨下行到胯，胯亦會自動調節方位來減少震動，平衡身體。

你只要拳架規整，雙魚順暢，就有絕地反擊的可能性。

5. Double Fish Ring in Lu-style Xinyi

All the actions of Lu-style Xinyi are done during moving. Striking also happens during the moving. We call it a Living Technique, which says that attacking by a mistake is rather than missing an attacking. Box like water is slowly spreading; attack like the body is burning. In a word, finish the three turns and nine changes in one movement. The reason to startle a spirit like water is that it is fast and unpredictable, which comes from the movement of the hip and the spine.

The power comes from the back foot pressing on the ground. Expand the joint by twisting and turning as if folding and opening a fan, so that the power is delivered from foot to the knee, then to the crotch. The crotch adjusts the angles and direction of the force during the movement in order to keep the body upright and balanced like a car swerving on a curve road; only, the curve itself has a slanted surface, one side being thicker than the other. This makes it safer, and is what we mean when we say: walk with the hip, and box with the hip.

You can get different circles in different angles by turning the hips. The force follows the hips to the third, fourth, fifth bone of the spine and turn around there. In detail, the movement of the transverse muscles of the waist drive the third, fourth, fifth bone of the spine to rotate (some people hurt themselves at the place. try to keep the waist upright). It also drives the blood and energy to flow with purposes, and turn the forces into strength.

The bigger the hip's angle is, the greater the strength; the faster the speed is, the greater the strength produced and the deeper the power will be released. If the hip is rotated levelly, the force in the third, fourth, fifth bone of the spine moves in a path of the shape of "C". If the hip is rotated diagonally, the force moves in a path of the shape of "S" or "8".

The circle made by the turn of the hip, the "S" of the spine, and the "S" made by the force and strength altogether form Double Fish Ring in Lu-style Xinyi. It is a three-dimensional and changing movement.

When attacked by an external force, defend with an intention. When the external force moves through the point of contact to the spine, swing the spine to the left or right to lead the force away. Use the middle section of the hip to move upward or downward to redirect the force, which is the function of Double Fish Ring in Lu-style Xinyi.

When you are suddenly attacked by an external force and

it is too late to defend, the external force reaches the spine through the point of contact, but the "S" shape in the spine could dodge it automatically and partially redirect it. The rest of the force might go along the spine down to the hip, where the hip can also automatically redirect it to reduce shock and rebalance the body.

As long as your boxing frame is right and Double Fish Ring is running smoothly, you will have opportunity to counter even in a desperate situation.

盧式心意・排打

Lu Style Xinyi Impacting or Linear Striking'

（Pai Da）

一、磕肘

磕肘是練習小臂的抗擊打承受能力。沾實於腕下小臂前半部分兩側的皮抱骨處（尺骨、橈骨），而不是兩側的肉厚處。兩臂撐拔屈折成形，肘處內折170度，腕亦內折，如一把彎刀，大拇指側如是刀背，刀走背多是用挑、掛二藝，小拇指側如是刀刃，刀走刃多是用劈、削二藝，善用刀者多用刀下一把處（刀尖後移），肘也是。

可一人對椿練習，但最好是二人對磕練習。有活步、定步二藝。兩臂屈折、伸拔與身體形成90度夾角，以脊骨為軸心，左轉右旋，輔以熊膀的開合，完成挑、掛、劈、削，但內裡都有一個搓藝（以左手為例）。

1. Ke Zhou （Knocking with Forearms）

"Knocking with Forearms" is a method for practicing forearms fighting. Knock against each other with the first half of the
forearm（the part close to the wrist）. Arch the arm and bend
the elbow to approximately 170 degrees. Turn the wrists inward.
The arm looks like a curved knife, the side of the thumb will
be the back of the knife, which is used for Blocking（Tiao）or
Parrying（Gua）. The side of the little finger will be the edge of
the knife, which is used for Chopping（Pi）or Scraping（Xiao）.
Those who are good at knives use the first part of a knife, which
is the knifepoint, "Knocking with Forearms" does this as well.

You can practice "Knocking with Forearms" against a pole,
but it is better to practice with a person. You can practice it
with moving steps or without moving. Bend and stretch both
arms to form a 90 degree angle to the body. Use the spine as an
axis to turn your body left or right. Practice Blocking（Tiao）or
Parrying（Gua）with Bear Shoulders（Xiong Bang）, chopping
（Pi）and scraping（Xiao）, and the technique of rubbing
（Cuo）. Here we use the left hand as an example.

路上人多君子少，山上石多金子稀。寧可失傳，不可亂傳，傳要眞傳。

插劍式

以把護腹，襠內裏、內掛或內挑、內磕，約與胯高。把走乾六、坎一、艮八，肘走兌七、中五、震三。

Cha Jian（Insert the Sword Into the Scabbard）

One hand（Ba）protects the abdomen. Turn the knees inward. Knock with forearm at the level of the hip, parrying or blocking.

The hand goes to Qian 6（see the figure at the section of "Boxing Frame, Moving Path and Spirit"）, Kan 1, and Gen 8. The elbow moves accordingto the Dui 7, Zhong 5, and Zhen 3.

雞腿搖閃勢難當，龍形裹橫緊相連；遊蝶穿花蛇撥草，拱手含額猴豎蹲。

3

4

5

6

拔劍式

以把護腹，襠外裏、外劈或外削、外磕，約與胯高。把走艮八、坎一、乾六，肘走震三、中五、兌七。

Ba Jian（Pullout the Sword from the Scabbard）

One hand（Ba）protects the abdomen. Turn the knees out-ward. Knock with forearm at the level of the hip, chopping or scraping. The hand goes to Gen 8, Kan 1, and Qian 6. The elbow moves the Zhen 3, Zhong 5, and Dui 7.

虎抱頭式

以把護腮，胸外裹、外劈或外削、外磕，約與鼻高。把走巽四 、離九 、坤二 ，肘走震三、中五 、兌七 。

Hu Bao Tou(Tiger Embraces His Head)

One hand（Ba）protects the cheek. Push the chest outward. Knock with forearm at the level of the hip, chopping or scraping. The hand goes to Xun 4, Li 9, and Kun 2. The elbow moves according to the Zhen 3, Zhong 5, and Dui 7.

1   2

黃龍擺尾三斜式，左右相顧裹邊炮；雲遮月把天地暗，丹鳳朝陽把翅展。

猴形小裏斜裡落，縱橫十字回身攀；狸貓上樹蛇捆身，猛虎擺尾中節斷。

5

6

貓洗臉式

以把護腮，胸內裹、內掛或內挑、內磕，約與胯高。把走坤二、離九、巽四，肘走兌七、中五、震三。

Mao Xi Lian ShiCat Was（hes His Face）

One hand（Ba）protects the cheek. Draw the chest inward. Knock with forearm at the level of the hip, parrying or blocking. The hand goes to Kun2, Li 9, and Xun4. The elbow moves according to the Dui 7, Zhong 5, and Zhen 3.

3

4

5

6

二、鬥 肩

鬥肩又稱抗膀子，或叫擠油。擠油是一個形象的
說法，說的是過去作坊裡榨油時，掄大錘砸木鍥咚咚
作響；又像現在打樁機打樁時現場的咚鳴響，震撼有
力。

鬥肩要的就是撞擊時的結實有力，盤的是熊膀的
開合貫通如一和腰馬的合順與驚鴻。

可一人對樁練習，但最好是二人鬥肩。有活步、
定步二藝。鬥肩沾實有三：前肩、側肩（正肩）、後
肩（以左肩例）。

2. Dou Jian (Fighting with Shoulders)

It is known as 'Kang Bang Zi', or "Squeeze Oil" (Ji You).
Originally, "Squeeze Oil" came from the way that the old work-
shops used mash-hammers to make oil, with the sounds of "Dong
Dong". It is also like a sound from a pile-hammer. Here we use
it to represent that the fighting force shocks people.

Fighting with Shoulders needs a strong and powerful force.
Practice it with Bear Shoulders (Xiong Bang).

You can use a pole to practice against, but it is better to
practice with a person. You can practice it with moving steps or
without moving. You can use the front shoulder, the side shoul-

豈知悟得嬰兒頑，打法天下是眞形。內名守洞塵技藝，外呼心意六合拳。

der (Zheng Jian), or the back of the shoulder to fight.

Here we use the Left hand as an example.

鬥前肩

主要沾實肩膀的正面部分，練習塌中節。肩與胯合，合而塌。力走坤二、中五、艮八。

1

Fighting with the Front Shoulders

It is used to exercise the front part of the shoulder and to sink the middle section. The shoulders and hips are unified and sunken. The force goes to Kun2, Zhong 5, and Gen 8.

2

十二大形河北派，十大眞形河南邦；人比花開滿樹紅，到老能有幾個成。

盧式心意六合拳開拳

可嘆先輩相傳苦，今承衣鉢那兒人。

鬥正肩

主要沾實肩膀的側面部分，練習折中節。肩與胯合，合而折。力走坤二、兌七、乾六。

Fighting with the Side of the Shoulder

It is used to exercise the side of the shoulder and to bend the middle section. The shoulders and hips are unified and bent. The force goes to Kun2, Dui 7, and Qian 6.

從來散之必有其統也，分之必有其合也，以故天地間四面八方。

盧式心意六合拳開拳

鬥後肩

主要沾實肩膀的後面部分，練習甩中節。肩與胯
合，開而甩。力走巽四、離九、坤二。

鬥肩有一個二人遊戲：遊戲時，兩個人只可沾實
肩與胯，手與臂不能用。左手握右手腕或右手握左手
腕，置於腹前或放於背後。方寸之地畫一個圓，約二
個平方，過去是在石碾之上或八仙桌上。就這麼一個
地方，誰出圈或掉下來誰輸。鬥時可虛可實，可領可
讓，可引而空，也可引而實。學會了鬥肩也就學會了
中節出勁。

Fighting with the Back of the Shoulder

It is used to exercise the back of the shoulder and to swing
the middle section. The shoulders and hips are unified and
swung. The force goes to Xun 4, Li 9, and Kun 2.

There is a game for "Fighting with Shoulders". In this
game, two persons use their shoulders and hips only, not their
hands or arms. The left hand holds the right wrist, or vice versa.
Place both hands at the abdomen or behind the body. Draw a
circle on the ground that the size is about two square meters. In
olden times, people practiced it on the top of a stone table or on
the top of an old-fashioned square table. The one who is forced
out of the circle or falls from the table loses. When fighting, it

can be empty or solid, leading or following. Lead him empty or
lead him solid. Once you have learned "Fighting with Shoulder", you will know how to use the force of the middle section.

1

2

三、排 身

一人對椿練習是鯉魚打挺和狸貓上樹二藝，兩人排身有定步和活步之分。定步，多用寸步、活步，可雞步也可蛇形調步。主要是練習內腑的抗擊打承受能力。初時要慢、輕，逐步加力。沾實一點時要發聲：噎、嘿、哈、嗥……在呼一半時沾實；有一定承受能力後，可嘗試著在吸氣一半時沾實。瞬間的鼓實與吸實，可使體內的氣壓增大，血氣充實，護住內腑。但不可以長時間地鼓實與吸實，因為缺氧。排身有二藝：直排身和側排身。

以身體的中心線來分割，人體可以分有兩部分，左側和右側。左側含左臉、左胸、腹部左側、胯的左半部分、左手和左腿；右亦然。排身只沾實一側的胸、腹、胯三個部分。

3. Pai Shen（Knocking the Body）

When you practice "Knocking the Body" by using a pole (Zhuang), use Carp Jump Stance (Li Yu Da Ting), Palm Cat Climbs a Tree Stance (Li Mao Shang Shu), Moving Steps, or Staying Steps. The Moving Steps are the Inch Step, Chicken Step (Ji Bu), or the Snake Shaped Steps (She Xing Bu). This movement is used to strengthen the internal organs. At the beginning, practice it slowly and gently, and then increase the power gradually. When the body is knocked, pronounce Yi, Hei, Ha, Hao. When you exhale half way, knock. After the knocking ability is increased, you can try to knock when you inhale half way. The instance of bulging could increase the body pressure and make the blood and Qi enriched to protect the internal organs. But be careful, because if you hold your breath too long, it may cause a shortage of oxygen.

There are two ways of Knocking the Body: Straight Knocking and Side Knocking.

From the center line of the body, the human body is divided into a left side and a right side. The left side includes: the left part of the face, the left part of the chest, the left part of the abdomen, left hip, left hand, and left leg. The right side includes: the right part of the face, the right part of the chest, the right part of the abdomen, right hip, right hand, and right leg. Knock with the Chest, abdomen, and hips, either the right side or the left side.

上欲動而下自隨之，下欲動而上自領之，上下動而中部應之，中部動而上下和之。

盧式心意六合拳開拳

直排身

開弓放箭式、夾剪之式，三尖照，抬左手，進左腿，二人兩把掌心相貼，上舉過肩過頭，寸步進中門，沾實於左胸、左腹、左胯，碰撞有聲；右亦然。

Straight Knocking

Use postures: Draw a Bow, Clip and Cut, and Three Points in Accordance. Raise the left hand. The left leg takes a step forward. Two persons touch by their palms at a height that is over their shoulders or heads. Inch Step to place the left foot between the opponent's feet. Then knock with the left side. The right side does the same.

1

2

3

4

5

側排身

寶劍出鞘式、夾剪之式，三尖照，抬右手，進左腿，龍折身，雙肩一陰近一陽，雙把上舉過肩過頭，側身，寸步側插，沾實於肩，肩下正側面肋部、肋下腰，腰下胯，碰撞有聲；右亦然。

Side Knocking

Use postures: Sword Out of the Scabbard, Clip and Cut, and Three Points in Accordance, Raise the right hand. Take a step forward with the left leg. Dragon Bends (Long Zhe Sheng). One shoulder is Yin, another one is Yang. Raise both hands over the shoulders and the head. Inch Step sideways to place

1

the left foot between the opponent's feet. Then knock with shoulders and the ribs which are under the left side of the shoulder, the waist under the ribs, and the hip under the waist, pronouncing Yi, Hei, Ha, Hao. The right side does the same.

當時而靜，寂然湛然，居其所而穩如泰山；

4

5

四、二人攻防

1. 虎抱頭

一人打，裹邊炮，高邊腿。一人防，手不離腮，以聳肩或上搓護頭；肘不離肋，沉肩下頂，護胸，防守左右來拳和腿。龍折身，雙肩一陰返一陽，亦可協防中路。

2. 貓洗臉

一人打，當頭炮，臥地炮，正蹬腿。一人防，肘不離肋，手不離腮，以熊膀的開合貫通如一防守來拳和腿，把防頭、肘防肋，合胸關門。開胸亦可協防左右。

3. 寒雞尋食

一人打，正蹬腿，低邊腿。一人防，磨脛、拎腿、頂膝，防守來腿與拳，磨脛進襠，擠走直線，踩中門。拎腿有掛藝，橫來豎掛，直來橫掛。頂膝有轉藝，向前進有三條路：左頂、右頂、前頂。

4. Offense and Defense

(1) Hu Bao Tou (Tiger Embraces His Head)

One person attacks via a Wrapping Side Cannon (Guo Bian Pao) or High Side Kick (Gao Bian Tui). Another person defends by putting hands on the cheek, raising shoulders, or twisting up to protect the head. Elbow against ribs, sink shoulders to protest the chest. Block the attack from the other's fist or legs. Dragon Bends (Long Zhe Sheng). The shoulders roll over to exchange Yin and Yang, which also blocks the attack of the middle.

(2) Mao Xi Lian (Cat Washes His Face)

One person attacks via a Straight Cannon (Dang Tou Pao), Lying Cannon (Wuo Di Pao), or direct kicking. Another person defends it by elbow against the ribs, putting hands on the cheek, and using the Bear Shoulders (Xiong Bang) to block the fist or leg from the attack. Hands protect head and elbows protect ribs. Draw the chest in as if closing a door. Push the chest out to protect the left or the right side.

(3) Han Ji Xun Shi (Chicken Seeking Food in the Cold)

One person attacks via a direct kick on the lower body of the opponent (Di Bian Tui). Another person defends it by rubbing the lower leg, lifting the leg, or pushing the knee up to block the incoming leg or fist. While rubbing the lower leg, step forward in a straight line to the middle between the opponent's feet. Lift the leg with an intention of a parry. Block a vertical attack by a horizontal parry; block a horizontal attack by a vertical parry. Push the knee up with an intention of turning. There are three ways to step forward: pushing up to the left, pushing up to the right, and pushing up to the front.

動無不動，前後左右並無抽扯游移之形。

盧式心意・十形

Lu-Style Xinyi. Ten Big Forms

盧式心意六合拳開拳

一、雞形・搓把

雞形下式

搓把

鷹捉把

雞有欺鬥之勇。搓把有二把藝，兩個字：一是脫藝，逃脫的脫。力走坎一、中五、離九。二是抓藝，抓住的抓。力走離九、中五、坎一。起落順直勁。

雞形下式

開弓放箭式、夾剪之式，三尖照。肩有前後之分，把亦有上下前後之分，前把在上，大拇指朝外，中指朝上，小臂約垂直於地面，大臂約平行於地面。後把在下，虎口抵在前把的肘尖外。

搓　把

後把沿前把的手臂外側上搓，把心朝裡，虎口朝上，止於鼻高。後把變前把上把，原前把以肘尖為鋒下爭，抵在現前把的腕下內側。

脫　藝

爭脫逃掉之意。寸步起，後把繞過前把成前把，沿原前把的若火雞之內攻，發之而不及掩耳。

鷹捉把

雞搓把

手臂外側上搓，把心朝裡，虎口朝上，止於鼻高。後把以肘尖為鋒下爭，抵在現前把的腕下內側。

托 藝

托物不許下落之意。寸步落。

抓 把

雙把暗合，後把內翻而出，變為前把，中指朝前，把心朝下，止於鼻高。原前把內翻而下，壓在前把的腕上，過步而起，單腿支撐。後把壓前把，前把抓而下，止於臍高。過步而落，落要踩，束身下就，墊步。

週而復始。搓把和抓把合二為一，以前把肩為圓心，過後肩，過腮，成於雞形下式。

【用法】

（1）一手上搓，搓掉中路來拳，後手隨勢上沖，拳是沖天炮，沾實於對手的腹、胸、下頦，肘亦可。

（2）連續兩手上搓，掃清中路來拳，後手翻上崩，用拳背上擊，起手打襠，抬手打臉，繼而下抓對手的面門。

Cuo Ba (Twisting Hold)
1. Chicken Forms · Twisting Hold

Chickens are deceivingly brave when fighting. Twisting Hold (Cuo Ba) includes two skills: one is escaping (Tuo), which force goes to Kan 1, Zhong 5, and Li 9. The other is 「grabbing」 (Zhua), which force goes to Li 9, Zhong 5, and Kan 1.

Chicken Form– Low Stance

Drawing a Bow stance, Clip and Cut stance, and Three Points in Accordance. Shoulders: one is ahead of the other, we call them the front shoulder and the back shoulder respectively. Hands: one is ahead of the other, we call them the front hand and the back hand respectively; one is higher then another, we call them the high hand and the low hand respectively. The front hand is the high hand, thumb pointing outward, middle finger pointing upward, forearm perpendicular to the ground, upper arm almost paralleling to the ground. The back hand is the low hand, the Tiger Mouth (the point between the thumb and the index finger) touches the elbow tip of the front hand.

Cuo Ba (Twisting Hold)

The back hand rubs the front hand along the outside of the arm, palm facing inward and Tiger Mouth facing upward at the height of the nose. The back hand becomes a front hand and the high hand. Push the elbow of the new back hand (the original front hand) downward. The back hand supports the inside of the wrist of the front hand.

"Escaping Skill" means having the intention to escape. Starting with Inch Step, the back hand bypasses the front hand and becomes a new front hand. The back hand rubs upward along the outside of the arm of the front hand, palm facing inward and Tiger Mouth facing upward at the height of the nose. Push the elbow of the back hand (the original front hand) downward. The back hand supports the inside of the wrist of the front hand.

"Supporting Skill" means to keep an object from falling. Inch Step falls behind.

Zhua Ba (Grabbing Hold)

The Two hands hide correspondingly. The back hand turns over inwardand then outward, becoming the front hand, the middle finger pointing to the front, palm facing downward at the height of the nose. The original front hand turns over inwardand downwardly, and presses to the wrist of the new front hand. The step passes through as well as upwards, the body is supported by a single leg. The back hand presses the front hand. The front hand grabs downwardly and stops at the height of the navel. The step passes through and stamps, tightening and lowering the body, then Skip Step.

Repeat above movements. Coordinate the "Twisting Hold" (Cuo Ba) and the "Grabbing Hold" (Zhua Ba) as one. Use the shoulder of the front hand as an axis, the front hand passes the shoulder and the lower cheek to form the Chicken Form–Low Stance.

Usage

(1) One hand twists upward and drops to block an attacking fist from the middle. The other hand (back hand) punches opponent's abdomen, chest, chin, or elbow with Punch Upward Cannon.

(2) Two hands twist upward continuously, clearing away the incoming fist from the central line. The back hand turns over, rising hands strike the opponent's crotch and face with the back of the fists. Then both hands also grab his forehead.

1

盧式心意六合拳開拳

5 6
7 8

二、鷂形・鷂子入林

鷂形入林（一）

鷂形入林（二）

鷂形下式

鷂有側翅之能，可以自由穿梭在茂密的樹林裡，不傷及羽毛。見其形取其意，束身而起，側身而去，翻身而走。行拳時有三法：一是單樁，圍繞著一個圓形來打拳；二是雙樁，圍繞著兩個圓形，沿著「8」字形來打拳，會「8」字形打拳，就會四面八方地打拳；三是沿波紋形打拳，走「～～～」線。起落縱橫勁。力走坤二、離九、巽四或巽四、離九、坤二。

鷂形下式

兩腿站立，膝微屈，腳有前後之分，前腳腳後跟著地，前腳抬，後腳平，重心落在後腿上。三尖照。肩有前後之分，前把肘與臍合，把在異側胯旁，把刃朝外，插劍式，後把屈折成形，肘不離肋，中指朝上，把心朝裡，置於耳旁，約與額高。

盧式心意六合拳開拳

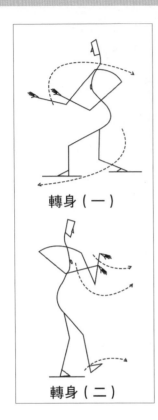

轉身（一）

轉身（二）

入林把

開弓放箭式、夾剪之式，三尖照。雙把暗合走橫勁，上把翻而把心朝下，內掛內裏，下把轉而上抄，把心朝上，內掛外裏，下把裏而前，上把抵在下把的腕下。寸步。

翻身把

身體以前腳為圓心180度轉動，起橫勁。以後腳跟退行過步，右腳前逆時針，左腳前逆時針。肩膀隨身轉，雙肩膀一陰返一陽，雙把暗合，把心相對下搓驚起，以身帶把。手腳齊到方為真。

入林把、翻身把週而復始。

【用法】

（1）前手外掛，後手當頭炮或臥地炮，身前切，轉身用肘或拳背甩擊，另一手隨勢裏邊炮。

（2）前手當頭炮，後手前掛，身前切，轉身用肘或拳背上撩，多打襠，另一手隨勢沖天炮加提膝。

2. Yao Zi Ru Lin（Sparrow–hawk Form · Sparrow–hawk Enter the Forest）

Sparrow–hawks can open their wings sideways and shuttle into the thickly wooded forest freely, without hurting their feathers. Take the way that Sparrow–hawks fly and tighten your body, turning and walking sideways. There are three ways to practice it: the first is using a single pole and practicing around it; the second is using two poles, and practicing around the poles with an "8" shaped path, which makes you able to fight in all directions; the third is to follow a wavy line, such as: the shape of "∼∼∼". The energy is delivered horizontally or vertically, up or down. The force goes to Kun 2, Li 9, and Xu 4; or Xu 4, Li 9 and Kun 2.

Sparrow–hawk Form – Low stance

Stand on both legs. Bend the knees slightly, one foot (front foot) ahead of the other (back foot). Lift the front foot and keep the heel on the ground. The back foot is flat on the ground. The weight is on the back foot. Three Points in Accordance. The elbow of the front hand coordinates to the navel, the hand by the other side of the hip, the edge of the front hand facing outward; Insert the Sword Into the Scabbard. The back arm bends, the elbow touching the ribs, middle finger pointing up, palm facing inward by the ear at the height of the forehead.

Ru Lin Ba (Entering Forest Hold)

Draw a Bow stance; Clip and Cut stance; Three Points in Accordance. Both hands are in coordination and the force goes horizontally. The palm of the high hand turns over and faces downwards; Parry Inward; Wrap Around Inward. The low hand turns over and lifts, palm facing upward. Parry Inward and Wrap Around Outward. The low hand wraps around forward. The low hand supports the wrist of the high hand. Inch Step.

Fan Shen Ba (Turning Over Body Hold)

Pivoting on the front foot, turn the body 180 degrees. The force goes horizontally. Use the heel of the back foot as a cutting edge; the step passes through. The right foot turns counter-clockwise, the left foot turn counter-clockwise. The shoulders roll over to exchange Yin and Yang, two hands in coordination, palms facing each other and twisting downward. The body leads the hands. Hands and feet move at the same time.

Repeat: Entering Woods (Ru Lin Ba); Turning Over Body Hold (Fan Shen Ba)

Usage

（1）The front hand swings outward. The back hand does a Straight Cannon（Punch Straight at the Head）（Dang Tou Pao）or a Lying Cannon（Wuo Di Pao）. Turn the body to whip by the elbow or the back of one fist. The other hand does a Swinging Cannon（Guo Bian Pao），

（2）The front hand does a Straight Cannon（Punch Straight at the Head）（Dang Tou Pao）. The back hand parries forward. Lean one side of the body forward. Then turn the body and lift the elbow or the back of one fist to hit his crotch. The other hand does Punch Upward Cannon and the knee on the same side is lifted.

吸則為陰，呼則為陽。主乎靜者為陰，主乎動者為陽。

盧式心意六合拳開拳

1

2

3

4 5
6 7

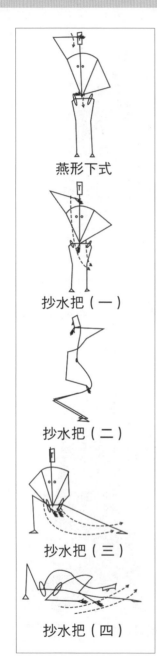

燕形下式

抄水把（一）

抄水把（二）

抄水把（三）

抄水把（四）

三、燕形·燕子抄水

燕有抄水之妙。驚起驚落，一貫勁直。力走坎一、中五、離九。

燕形下式

開弓放箭式，兩腿並立，膝微屈，側身，雙把握拳，上拳抵在眉衝處（前額正中稍下），大拇指朝下，拳心朝外；下拳抵氣海處（臍下），大拇指朝上，拳心朝裡，左右拳大拇指上下對應，上把上提，下把下沉，撐拔脊椎骨，節節拔起、順直。

抄水把

屈膝下蹲，保持身體中正，雙把同時翻轉下落，由拳變把，中指朝下，大拇指朝外，沿人體中線下抄。屈膝至極正側方搓地出腳，左把在下出左腳，右手在下出右腳，重心坐在後腿上。把隨身落，雙把在襠前轉、襠下合，大拇指朝上，把心相對，前抄，腳貼地搓，把貼地抄，雙把止於前腳上。

鑽天把

轉胯，後腿撐而起，前腳以跟為圓心轉而前，肩隨胯轉90度，重心移到前，前腿撐而蹬，雙把沿弧線上抄，前把止於眉高，後把抵在前把的腕下內側。墊步。

週而復始：過步轉身90度，雙把轉而翻，鼻前分而爭，前把下爭而後把上爭，呈燕形下式，抄水把、鑽天把，左右調步。

【用法】

（1）雙把塌而前行，雙把上搓對手的面門或胸。

（2）雙把塌而前行，用手指直戳對手的面門或喉。

（3）雙把塌而前行，雙把上搓，用肘沾實對方的胸或肋下。

3. Yan Zi Chao Shui（Swallow Taking up Water）

Swallows takes up water, suddenly rising and suddenly falling, with straight force. The force goes to Kan 1, Zhong 5, and Li 9.

Swallow Form – Low Stance

Drawing a Bow stance. Stand with both legs next to each

other; bend the knees slightly. The body is sideways. Turn both hands into fists, the upper fist at the Meichong (the center of the forehead and slightly close to the eyebrows), thumb pointing downward, and palm facing outward. The lower fist is at the Qihai (the place below the navel), thumb pointing upward, and palm facing inward. Both thumbs are facing each other. Lift the high hand and sink the low hand. Stretch all the bones of the spine, one by one lifting along upright.

TChao Shui Ba (aking Up Water Hold)

Lower the body and keep it upright. Both fists turn over and move downward at the same time. Then turn both fists into opening hands, middle fingers pointing downward, thumbs pointing outward. Both hands move downward. Bend the knees and slide a foot outward; if the left hand is the low hand, than slide the left foot outward; if the right hand is the low hand, than slide the right foot outward. The weight is on the back leg. The hands fall with the body and turn over in front of the crotch, coordinating under the crotch, thumbs pointing up, palms facing each other. Grab forward. Feet rub the ground, hands grab close to the ground. Both hands stop over the front foot.

Zhuan Tian Ba (Drill or Fly into the Sky Hold)

Turn the hip, the back leg stretches and lifts. Pivoting on the heel of the front foot, the foot turns forward. The shoulder follows the hip to turn 90 degrees. Shift the weight to the front leg. The front leg stretches and kicks. Both hands grab upward in an arc. The front hand stops at the height of the eyebrows; the back hand supports the inside of the wrist of the front hand, then Skip Step.

Repeat: Pass Through Step; turn the body 90 degrees. Both hands turn over and separate in front of the nose; Push the front hand downward and the back hand upward to perform Swallow Form Low Stance; Taking up Water (Chao Shui Ba); Drilling into the Sky (Zhuan Tian Ba). Adjust the feet.

Usage

(1)Both hands sink and move forward to twist the face or chest of the opponent .

(2)Both hands sink and move forward to stab directly the face or throat of the opponent.

(3)Both hands sink and move forward to twist upward. Elbows hit the chest or ribs of the opponent.

氣不能無陰陽，即所謂人不能無動靜，鼻不能無出入。

氣不能無陰陽，即所謂人不能無動靜，鼻不能無出入。

158

盧式心意六合拳　開拳

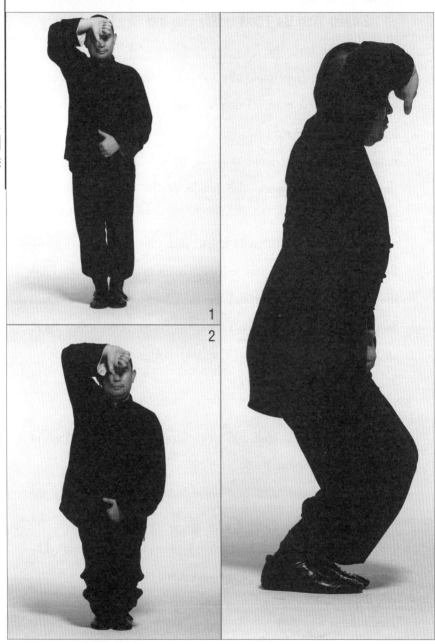

1

2

盧式心意六合拳開拳

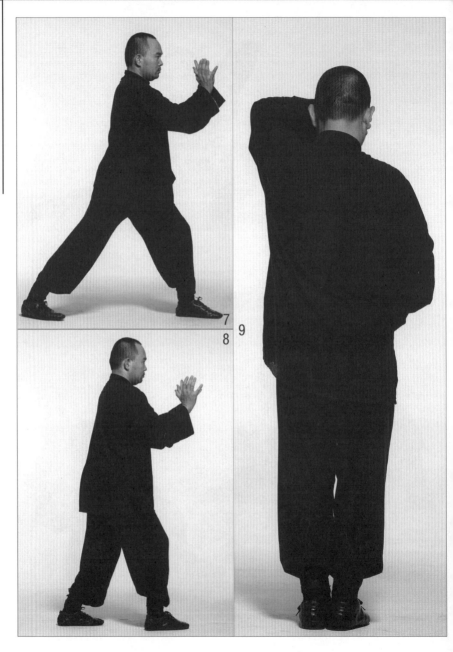

7
8
9

四、鷹形・大劈挑領

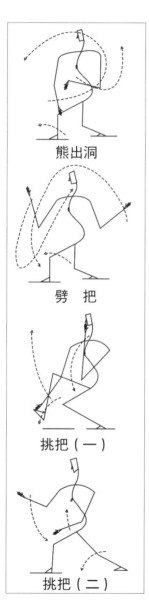

熊出洞

劈　把

挑把（一）

挑把（二）

鷹有捉拿之功，鷹的狠毒決絕如板斧闊刀，挑而上、劈而下。盧師曰：「前面是座山也要給我劈開半拉來，前面是座嶺也要給我挑翻它。」起落勁。劈力走離九、中五、坎一；挑力走坎一、中五、離九。

劈　把

熊出洞下式。開弓放箭式，夾剪之式，三尖照。前把以肩為圓心，以把為鋒，逆時針畫圓而上，過肩過耳，劈而下，前落，約與臍高。後把亦以肩膀為圓心沿弧線逆時針而上，過肩過耳，寸步。雙肩一陽返一陰，上把劈而下，束身下落，就成一團，過步提膝，肘貼膝，把貼足，單腿支撐，膝內折小於90度。

原下把翻而上，止在耳旁，把不離腮，肘不離肋，把心朝裡，在異側。

挑 把

開弓放箭式，牮杆之式，三尖照。前腳落而踩，前把挑而上，約止於肩高，中指朝前，大拇指朝上。後把翻而下，約止於襠前，把心朝下，中指朝前。

前把翻而下，後把抬而上，墊步，呈熊出洞下式，週而復始。

【用法】

（1）前手撥，後手劈，把劈頭，肘蓋臉，順直而下，繼而挑襠。

（2）前手劈臉，後手灌耳，前手不落後落，繼而挑對手大臂下方。

（3）前手撥，後手劈，劈對方出擊的大臂，順勢用肩沾實對手的胸。

4. Da Pi Tiao Ling（Great Split and Lift）

Eagles have an ability to grab with sharpness like a broadsword or an axe. Lift and split down. Master Lu sad："If there is a mountain in the front, split it into two pieces; if there is a ridge in the front, lift it up and turn it over". The force goes up and down. The chopping force goes to Li 9, Zhong 5, and Kan 1; the lifting force goes the Kan 1, Zhong 5, and Li 9.

Pi Ba（Splitting Hold）

Bear Exits its Den-Low Stance; Draw a Bow stance; Clip

and Cut stance; Three Points in Accordance. Using the front shoulder as an axis, and the hand as a sharp edge, the front hand turns counter-clockwise and draws a circle, passing the shoulder and the ear, splitting forward and downward at the level of the navel. The back hand, using the shoulder as an axis, follows an arc to turn counter-clockwise and up, passing the shoulder and the ear, then Inch Steps. The shoulders roll over to exchange Yin and Yang, the up hand splits down, contracting the body and dropping like a ball; Pass Through Step; lift the knee, with the elbow touching the knee, the hand touching the foot. The body is supported by a single leg, with the knee bending inward to form a less than 90 degree angle. The original lower hand turns over and stops by the ear. The hand does not leave the cheek; the elbow does not leave the ribs. The palm faces inward by the other side of the body.

Tiao Ba (Lifting Hold)

Draw a Bow stance; Prop Pole stance; Three Points in Accordance. The front foot stamps on the ground; the front hand lifts and stops at the height of the shoulder, middle finger pointing forward, thumb pointing down. The back hand turns over to the crotch, palm facing downward, the middle finger pointing forward.

Turn the front hand over and lift the back hand; Skip

盧式心意六合拳開拳

Step；Bear Exits its Den. Repeat above movements.

Usage

(1)The front hand pulls upward and the back hand splits his head, the elbow covering his face. The hand moves downward directly, then lifts up the crotch of the opponent.

(2)The front hand splits his face and the back hand hits his ear. The front hand is faster than the back hand to push up the upper arm of the opponent.

(3)The front hand pulls upward and the back hand splits the arm of the opponent, and takes an opportunity to use the shoulder to hit the chest of the opponent.

1

2

3

4

9

五、虎形・虎撲把

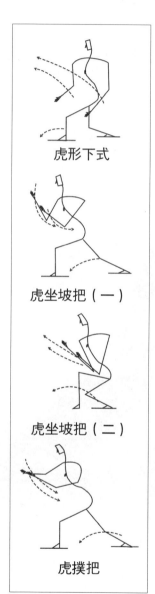

虎形下式

虎坐坡把（一）

虎坐坡把（二）

虎撲把

虎有撲食之勇。一個字「撲」，束身而下，就成一團，展身而起，丈二八尺，「束展二字一命亡。」起落順直勁。力走坎一、中五、離九。

虎形下式

開弓放箭式，夾剪之式，三尖照。挺胸而前，雙把暗合，把心相對，大拇指朝前，如持一把大槍在手，前把略高，後把略低。

虎坐坡把

龍折身，雙肩一陰返一陽，寶劍出鞘式，三尖齊。把隨肩走，後把變前把，兩把把心相對，大拇指朝上，束身、胸，起橫勁關門，寸步。束身而落，雙把內翻而落，左把逆時針，右把順時針，前把肘尖抵在自己的臍部，後把肘尖抵在自己的肋部，抵時有撞藝。墊步，重心擠在前腿上，束身下就成一團。

虎撲把

雙把落要撞，撞而起。過步，開弓放箭式，牟杆之式，三尖齊。展身而去，丈二八尺，後腿撐，前膝頂，雙把外翻搓而出，右把逆時針，左把順時針，雙把扣合，後把虎口頂在前把的大拇指後，折腕豎把（蝴蝶把），雙臂屈折成形約170度左右，向前進，雙把沾實。

週而復始：虎坐坡把，虎撲把，左右換步。

【用法】

（1）雙把塌而落，縮身而下，展身而起，雙把上搓對手的面門或胸。

（2）雙把塌而落，縮身而下，展身而起，用手指直戳對手的面門、喉、脅下。

5. Hu Pu Ba（Tiger Pouncing Hold）

Tigers are very fierce as they pounce on their food. The word "pouncing" means to tighten one's body first, then expand and jump up out eight or twelve feet. "Tightening and Expanding, two words take one life". The force goes up and down to Kan 1, Zhong 5, and Li 9.

Tiger Form–Low Stance

Draw a Bow stance; Clip and Cut stance; Three Points in Accordance. Stretch the chest and move forward. Both hands are in coordination, palms facing each other, thumbs pointing forward, as if holding a big spear. The front hand is higher than the back hand.

Hu Zuo Po Ba (Tiger Sitting on a Slope Hold)

Dragon Bends (Long Zhe Shen). The shoulders roll over to exchange Yin and Yang; Sword Out of the Scabbard stance; Three Points in Accordance. Both hands follow the shoulders; the back hand turns into the front hand, palms facing each other, thumbs pointing up. Tighten the body and the chest, the force goes horizontally; Inch Step. Tighten and sink the body. Both hands turn inward and sink; the left hand turns counter-clockwise; the right hand turns clockwise. Place the front hand on the navel and the back hand by the ribs, with intention to strike. Skip Step; maintain the weight on the front leg. Tighten the body like a ball.

Hu Pu Ba (Tiger Pouncing Hold)

Both hands sink and strike upward. Over Step; Draw a Bow stance; Prop Pole stance; Three Points in Accordance. Expand the body to jump out either 12 feet or 8 feet. Stretch the back leg, and push the front knee. Both hands turn over outward and twist out; the right hand turning counter-clockwise; the left hand turning clockwise. Both hands fastening together, the Tiger Mouth (the place between thumb and index finger) of the back hand touches the back of the thumb of the front hand. The wrist bends vertically to grasp (Butterfly Hold or Hu Dian Ba). Bend both arms approximately 170 degrees. Move forward and strike with both hands.

Repeat: Tiger Sitting on Slope Hold (Hu Zuo Po Ba), Tiger Pouncing Hold (Hu Pu Ba), with another foot.

Usage

(1) sink both hands, tighten and sink the body. Expand the body and jump up. Both hands twist on the face or chest of the opponent.

(2) sink both hands, tighten and sink the body. Expand the body and jump up. Stab with fingers to the face, the throat, or either side of the opponent.

至於氣之發動，要皆梢節動，中節隨，根節催之而已。

1　2

3　4

六、馬形·夜馬奔槽

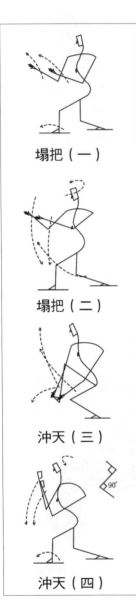

塌把（一）

塌把（二）

沖天（三）

沖天（四）

馬有奔騰之功，橫衝直撞，一往無前。起落順直勁。力走離九、中五、坎一。塌而落，奔而出，踩而起，運動中要有節奏感。

馬形下式

開弓放箭式，夾剪之式，三尖照。把有前後之分，雙把中指朝前，把心朝下，前把約與肩高，後把扶在前把的肘關節內側。

塌 把

寸步，雙把搓而前，抖勁，一如策馬抖韁，欲下先上。過步提膝，單腿支撐，膝內折小於90度，屈折成形。龍折身，雙肩一陰返一陽，束身下塌，雙把下捉，置於前腿的兩側，肘與膝合，把與足合。

沖天炮

後腿撐，前膝頂，身奔而

出，如洪之瀉。腳落而踩，雙把翻而上，力拔，如蹬靴。既而上沖，由把成拳，前把拳背朝外，約與鼻高，後把抵在前把的腕下內側。

週而復始：寸步腳內轉90度，同時轉身90度，塌把、沖天炮。

【用法】

雙把下塌出腳，正踢腿，腳落出拳，拳用沖天炮或當頭炮，沾實於對手的頭、胸、腹。

6. Ye Ma Ben Chao（Horse Form・Horses Rush to the Trough at Night）

The horse has the skill of galloping, running amuck with no stopping. The force goes up and down straight to Li 9, Zhong 5, and Kan 1. Gallop up and down with cadence.

Horse Form–Low Stance

Draw a Bow stance; Clip and Cut stance; Three Points in Accordance. One hand is ahead of the other, the middle fingers pointing forward, palms facing downward, the front hand at the approximately height of the shoulder, the back hand touches the inside the elbow joint of the front hand.

Ta Ba（Sinking Hold）

Inch Step, two hands rubbing forward, shaking, as if spurring the horse and shaking the halter, intent to go up but go down first. Over Step; lift the knee, supporting the body by single leg, the knee bending inward to form a less than 90 degree angle. Dragon Bends (Long Zhe Sheng); the shoulders roll over to exchange Yin and Yang. Tighten the body to sink. Both hands grasp downward and stop by the sides of the front leg. Elbows are corresponding with knees and hands are corresponding feet.

Chong Tian Pao (Punch Upward Cannon)

The back leg supports, the front knee pushes forward, with the body being like flooding water. The foot stomps. Both hands turn over and move upwardly, as if putting on a tight boot, and then rush upwards, both hands turning into fists. The back of the front hand faces outward at the height of the nose. The back hand supports the wrist of the front hand.

Repeat: Inch Step; turn the foot inward 90 degrees and turn the body 90 degrees at the same time. Sinking Hold; Punch Upward Cannon.

Usage

Both hands sink down, stepping forwards. Straight kick forwards. Punch out when the foot drops on the ground; Punch Upward Cannon or Straight Cannon (Punch Straight at the Head) (Dang Tou Pao), hitting the opponent's head, chest, or abdomen.

5

梢亦鳥可弗講，此特身之梢耳，而猶未及乎梢之梢也。

七、熊形・單把

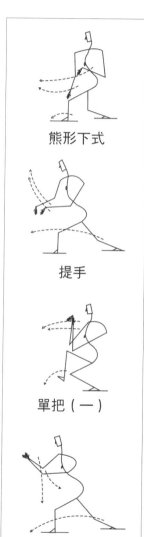

熊形下式

提手

單把（一）

單把（二）

熊有掀鼎之力。雙把扣合如一，兩膀開合貫通如一。肩催肘，肘催手，手中打抖擻，實為膀的開合抖擻。起落順直勁。力走乾六、兌七、坤二。

撩陰把

熊出洞。寸步，寶劍出鞘式，牮杆之式，三尖齊。把打頭落起手襠，起手撩陰，前把甩而出，把背朝外，後把扶在前把後。

提手把

過步提膝，單腿支撐，膝內折小於90度，屈折成形。雙把合而為一，以前把為主，後把抵在前把下，提而上磕，止於鼻高。開弓放箭式，三尖照。

單　把

後腿撐，前膝頂，身奔而出，如洪之瀉。腳落而踩，雙把扣合如一，肩催肘，肘催手，手四梢維何？發，其一也。夫發所繫，不列之於五行，無關於四體，似無足論矣。

中打抖擻，雙把扣合，後把虎口頂在前把的大拇指後，折腕豎把（蝴蝶把），雙臂屈折成形約170度，向前進，單把沾實。

週而復始：過步，雙把內翻而落，成熊形下式（輕步站）。

【用法】

前手撥，後手打，起手打襠，抬手打頭，翻手打胸，一順勢。

Dan Ba（Bear Form · Single Hold）

The bear has power to lift heavy weights. Both hands grasp as one, so do the shoulders. The shoulder pushes the elbow, the elbow pushes the hand, the hand strikes out shakily, which is actually the shoulder shakes by opening and closing. The force goes up and down to Qian 6, Dui 7, and Kun 2.

Liao Yin Ba (Lift the Genitals Up Hold)

Bear Exits its Den; Inch Step; Sword Out of the Scabbard stance; Prop Pole stance; Three Points in Accordance. One hand hits opponent's head and falls to Liao Yin Ba (lift up the genitals). The front hand swings, the back of the hand facing outward. The back hand supports the back of the front hand.

Ti Shou Ba (Lifting Hand Hold)

Over Step; lift the knee and support the body with a single leg. Bend the knee inward to form a less than 90 degree angle. Coordinate both hands as one. The front hand leads, the back hand supports the front hand. Lift both hands to knock at the height of the nose. Draw a Bow stance; Three Points in Accordance.

Dan Ba (Single Hold)

Stretch the back leg and press the front knee. The body rushes forward like flooding water. The feet stomp. Both hands coordinate as one. Shoulders press elbows; elbows press hands, hands shaking. The Tiger Mouth (the place between thumb and index finger) of the back hand touches the back of the thumb of the front hand. Bend the wrist to grasp vertically (Butterfly Hold or Hu Dian Ba). Bend both arms approximately 170 degrees. Move forward and strike with a hand.

Repeating: Over Step. Both hands turn over inwardand drop. Bear Form—Low Stance (Qin Bu Zhan or Light Step Stand)

Usage

The front hand pulls upward, and the back hand attacks. Lift one hand to hit opponent's crotch. Raise another hand to hit his head and take an opportunity to turn over the hand to hit his chest.

盧式心意六合拳開拳

5

6 7

盧式心意六合拳開拳

八、猴形・小裹

猴形下式

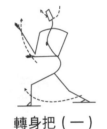

轉身把（一）

轉身把（二）

縱身把

　　猴有縱身之靈。漲身而起，縱身而前，縮身而落。裹物不露成其裹，圓中套圓，圈裡圈外，圓中見橫。起落縱橫勁，力走巽四、中五、乾六和坤二、中五、艮八。

猴形下式（猴豎蹲）

　　開弓放箭式，三尖照，夾剪之式。雙把暗合，把有上下前後之分，兩把前臂約與地面平行，前把在上約與臍高，後把在下稍低。屈膝下蹲，前腿大腿約與地面平行，小腿約與地面垂直，後腿屈折成形，膝內折小於90度，兩腿併一腿，距前腿約一拳。

轉身把

　　寸步，前把翻而上掛，大拇指朝上，止於鼻高。後把沿前把的肘外抄而上而搓，把心朝裡，食指朝上，漲身而起。過步，後腿過前腿時90度角轉身，左腿在後左轉，右腿在後右轉，雙肩一陰返一陽。開弓放箭式，三尖齊。

縱身把

過步提膝，單腿支撐，膝內折小於90度，屈折成形，墊步。寶劍出鞘式，三尖照。雙把暗合，翻而捉，捉而塌，有捉物迎膝之實。

週而復始：過步提膝後而落，束身，就成一團，寸步，腳外轉90度，左腳前左轉，右腳前右轉，墊步，成猴形下式。

【用法】

前手內裏，後手繼續接前手內裏，過步提膝，膝打密處人不知。

8. Hou Xing Xiao Guo（Monkey Form Small Wrapping Around）

Monkeys jump quickly. Expand the body and jump forward; tighten the body and fall. Wrap with no exposure to what is inside. Circles are within Circles and straight lines reside the circles. The force goes up and down, vertically and horizontally, to Xun 4, Zhong 5 , Qian 6, and Kun 2, Zhong 5, and Gen 8 .

Hou Xing Xia Shi or Hou Shu Dun（Monkey Form–Low stance）

Draw a Bow stance; Three Points in Accordance; Clip

and Cut stance. Both hands are coordinating; one hand is higher than the other; one hand is ahead of the other. Forearms are almost parallel to the ground. The front hand is higher at the height of the navel; the back hand is lower. Bend knees; the front leg is approximately parallel to the ground; the calf is about vertical to the ground. Bend the back leg inwards to be a less 90 degree angle. Two legs are apart about a fist in width.

Zhuan Shen Ba (Turning Body Hold)

Inch Step, the front hand turns and parries, thumb facing up at the height of the nose. The back hand twists up along the outside of elbow of the front hand, palm facing inward, the index finger pointing up, expanding the body and raising. Pass through Step. While the back leg passes the front leg, turn the body 90 degrees; if the left leg is the back leg, turn to the left; if the right leg is the back leg, turn to the right. The shoulders roll over to exchange Yin and Yang; Draw a Bow stance; Three Points in Accordance.

Zong Shen Ba (Jumping Body Hold)

Over Step, lift the knee, supported by a single leg, the knee bending inward to be a less than 90 degree angle. Skip Step; Sword Out of the Scabbard stance; Three Points in Ac-

cordance. Both hands are coordinating to "turn over and grasp"
or "grasp and sink", with intention of grasping and kicking
with a knee.

Repeat: Pass through Step; lift the knee and fall behind.
Tighten the body like a ball; Inch Step; The foot turns outward
90 degrees; if the left foot is in the front, turn to the left; if
the right foot is in the front, turn to the right, Skip Step; Monkey Form–Low Stance.

Usage

The front hand swings inwardly; the back hand follows the
front hand to wrap around inward. Pass through Step; lift the
knee. Hit a secret place by the knee without being noticed.

盧式心意六合拳開拳

1　2

3　4

今夫捶以言勢，勢以言氣。人得五臟以形成，即由五臟而生氣。

5

五臟實為性命之源，生氣之本，而名為心、肝、肺、腎是也。

6

7

九、蛇形・蛇撥草

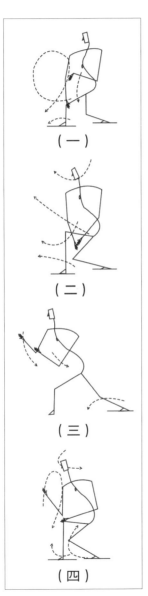

（一）

（二）

（三）

（四）

蛇有撥之能。起落勁，束身
下落，展身而起。圓中透著橫
勁，力走乾六、中五、巽四或艮
八、中五、坤二。前手撥草，後
手拔草，驚起驚落。

前手撥草把

熊形下式，前把以肩為圓
心，轉把上掛，約與鼻高，食指
朝上，內裹過頭下落，過肩止於
異側胯旁。後把抵在前把的腕
後，肩往後擰，束身下蹲，如蛇
捆身，愈團愈緊愈好，開弓放箭
式，三尖照，夾剪之式。

後手拔草把

後肩擰極而翻，雙肩一陰返
一陽，以脊柱骨為軸心，後把屈
折成形，肘內折約170度角，沿
直斜上方驚而出，後把變前把。
如蛇撲，以把心為鋒，把打肘
削，削中有蹭、蹭中有打，軌跡
中有滾有翻，一如揮一彎刀。原

前把繼續以肩為圓心，外掛外裏，過胯後上抬抵在前把的肘後。寶劍出鞘式，牮杆之式，三尖齊。寸步、墊步。後腿撐，前腿大步抄而前，大寸步，展身而起。前腿落後腿拖，墊步，一如犁地，縮身而落。

週而復始：寶劍出鞘式，夾剪之式，三尖齊。寸步，過步轉身，左腳在後左轉，右腳在後右轉，前手撥草式與後手拔草式。

【用法】

（1）前手撥，後手上沖，用把，沾實於鼻、下頦、胸、肋下。

（2）前手撥，後手上沖，用肘，沾實於對手的面門、胸、肋下。

9. She Bo Cao（Snake Stirs the Grass）

The snake has the ability to stir the grass. The force goes up and down, tighten the body and sink it; expand the body and raise it. The horizontal force hides in a circle to Qian 6, Zhong 5, and Xun 4, or Gen 8, Zhong 5, and Kun 2. The front hand stirs the grass, suddenly up and suddenly down.

Qian Shou Bo Cao Ba（Front Hand Stirs the Grass Hold）

Bear Form–Low Stance. Using the shoulder of the front

hand as an axis, the front hand turns over and parries at the height of the nose, the index finger pointing up. The front hand Wraps Around inwardly, passing the head, and stops at the other side of the hip. The back hand supports the back of the wrist of the front hand. The front shoulder twists backward. Tighten the body and squat the more the better, like a snake tightens itself. Draw a Bow stance; Three Points in Accordance; Clip and Cut stance.

Hou Shou Ba Cao Ba (Back Hand Stirs the Grass Hold)

The back shoulder twists and turns. The shoulders roll over to exchange Yin and Yang. Use the spine as an axis and bend the back elbow to approximately 170 degrees. Pull obliquely up suddenly. The back hand becomes a front hand. Pounce like a snake. Using the palm as a knife, the hand strikes and the elbow scraps. Twisting resides in the scraping and striking resides in twisting; move with rolling and turning, as if brandishing a curved knife. Use the shoulder as an axis, the original front hand continuously Parry Outward and Wrap Around Outward, passing the hip, and touches the elbow of the front hand. Sword Out of the Scabbard stance; Prop Pole stance; Three Points in Accordance; Inch Step; Pass through

Step. Stretch the back leg. The front leg strides forward, big Inch Step. Expand and raise the body. When the front leg drops, the back leg drags, Skip Step, as if plowing. Tighten the body and fall.

Repeat: Sword Out of the Scabbard stance; Clip and Cut stance; Three Points in Accordance; Inch Step; Skip Step. Turn the body, if the left foot is the back foot, then turn to the left; if the right foot is the back foot, then turn to the right. Stir the Grass with the Front Hand; Stir the Grass with the Back Hand.

Usage

(1)The front hand stirs, the back hand punches the nose, chin, chest or ribs of the opponent upwardly.

(2) The front hand stirs, the elbow of the back hand punches his face, chest or ribs upwardly.

盧式心意六合拳開拳

5　6

7

8

十、龍形・大龍形

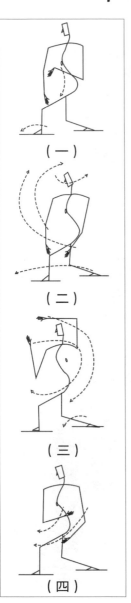

（一）

（二）

（三）

（四）

龍有搜骨之法。虛領頂勁，一個「掛」字，起落勁。龍行一波三折，一搖三晃，外有顛簸之形，內有搜骨之法，貫實於根，沾實於一。起落勁，力走坎一、中五、離九。起如浪翻，落如浪絕。

抱 把

熊出洞。開弓放箭式，三尖照之式。寸步，束身下蹲，後把下而抄，雙把暗合，把心相對，兩臂屈折成形，如抱一球或頑石。

起肘把

過步，踩。抱把成形不變，以肩為圓心順時針上行，前把上掛，過肩後，雙肩一陰返一陽為上把，置於頭頂上，把心朝下，小臂與地面平行，大臂約與地面垂直。原後把上抄為前把，把心朝裡，中指朝上，止於鼻高，小臂約與地面垂直，大臂約與地面平行。

落 把

墊步。抱把成形不變，以肩為圓心順時針下落，雙把把心相對，過頭、後肩之後，前把把心向下，過胯有抽搓之藝，後把下抄，把心朝上，過胯有抄捧之藝。

週而復始：抱把、起肘把、落把，左右調步。

【用法】

前手如抽刀般用把上削，後手用把隨勢用沖天炮，沾實對手的腹、胸、頭。後手亦可肘上掛。

10. Da Long Xing（Big Dragon）

Dragons have a method of moving their bones. Draw the head up. Parry with the force going up and down. The Dragon twists and moves with ups and downs, shaking and swinging. It moves like a wave on the outside, while inside its bones move, from the head to the tail. The force goes up and down to Kan 1, Zhong 5, and Li 9. Rise and fall as if surging.

Bo Ba（Holding a Ball Hold）

Bear Exits its Den; Draw a Bow stance; Clip and Cut stance; Three Points in Accordance; Inch Step. Tighten the body to squat. The back hand grabs downward. Both hands are coordinated, palms face each other. Both arms bend as if holding a ball or stone.

Qi Zhou Ba（Raise the Elbow Hold）

Pass through Step; stomp. Keep Holding a Ball no change.

Use the shoulder of the front hand as an axis, and the front hand parries clockwise. The shoulders roll over to exchange Yin and Yang. The front hand stops at the top of the head, palm facing down, forearm parallel to the ground, upper arm almost vertical to the ground. The original back hand becomes a front hand, palm facing inward, middle finger pointing up at the height of the nose, forearm almost vertical to the ground and upper arm almost parallel to the ground.

Luo Ba (Drop Hold)

Skip Step. Keep Holding a Ball no change, Use the shoulder of the front hand as an axis, and the front hand drops clockwise, palms facing each other. The front hand passes the head and the shoulder, palm facing downward. When it passes the hip, intend to rub. The back hand grabs downward, palm facing up. When it passes the hip, intend to grab.

Repeat: Holding a Ball; Raise the Elbow; Drop Hands; alter foot.

Usage

The front hand cuts upward as if taking a knife out of a scabbard. The back hand uses Punch Upward Cannon to hit the abdomen, the chest or the head of the opponent and also block his elbows.

1 2
3 4

盧式心意六合拳開拳

5

6 | 7

8 | 9

盧式心意六合拳開拳

盧式心意拳內功：九九之功

任督二脈為陰陽之海，人之脈比於水。故曰：脈之海。任者性也，凡人生育之本。脈起於中極之下，上毛際循腹而上咽喉至承漿而止，此陰脈之海；督脈者為陽脈之經網。尾閭背脊上玉枕、頂、額、鼻柱、人中到上橋止，為陽脈之海。

《金丹秘訣》曰：一擦一兜左右換手，九九之功，真陽不走。戌亥二時（戌時：晚上7：00至9：00，亥時：晚上9：00至11：00），為陰盛陽衰時，一手兜外陽，一手擦臍下（丹田），左右換手各八十一次，半月精固。李東垣曰：夜半收心靜坐片時，此生發周身元氣之大要也。

Lu Style Xinyi Neigong（Internal Power）:
the top internal power skills

There are many energy streams in the human body. Ren and Du are the major ones, which are like the seas, compared to the others, which are like water. They are also called the seas of Yin and Yang. Ren stream, the sea of Yin is in the front of the body, from the testicle where life comes from, goes up along the abdomen and throat, and stops at the ChengJiang (which is an acupuncture point located at the middle of the chin.) Du stream, the sea of Yan, in the back of the body, starts from coccyx and goes up along the spine, then pass the neck, the top of the head, the forehead, the nose, the Renchong (centre of the upper lip), and stops at Shangqiao (middle of the upper gum).

The trick is used to practice the internal power: one hand holds the testicle (for male), the other rubs the part under navel (Dantian), change hands after 81times at the time of Xu and Hai (pm 7:00~9:00 and pm 9:00~11:00), when Yin in the strongest and Yang in the weakest. The real Yang stays inside. Power will be improved in half month.

Li Dongyuan once said, "Concentrating the mind and sitting in peace at midnight is crucial for stimulating the energy of the body."

歡迎至本公司購買書籍

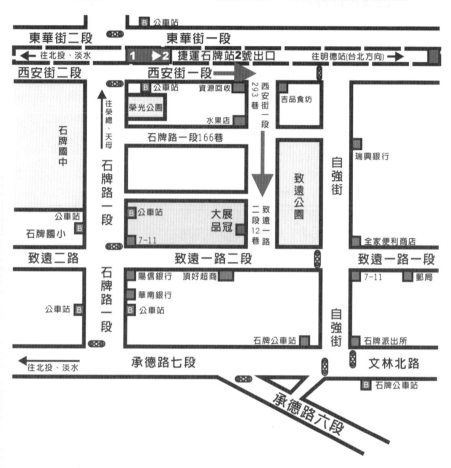

建議路線

1. 搭乘捷運‧公車

　　淡水線石牌站下車，由石牌捷運站2號出口出站(出站後靠右邊)，沿著捷運高架往台北方向走(往明德站方向)，其街名為西安街，約走100公尺(勿超過紅綠燈)，由西安街一段293巷進來(巷口有一公車站牌，站名為自強街口)，本公司位於致遠公園對面。搭公車者請於石牌站(石牌派出所)下車，走進自強街，遇致遠路口左轉，右手邊第一條巷子即為本社位置。

2. 自行開車或騎車

　　由承德路接石牌路，看到陽信銀行右轉，此條即為致遠一路二段，在遇到自強街(紅綠燈)前的巷子(致遠公園)左轉，即可看到本公司招牌。

國家圖書館出版品預行編目資料

盧式心意六合拳開拳／余江 著
——初版，——臺北市，大展，2017〔民106.06〕
面；21公分 ——（中英文對照武學；10）
ISBN 978－986－346－166－1（平裝：附影音光碟）
1.拳術 2.中國
528.972 106005340

盧式心意六合拳**開拳** 附VCD

著　　者／余　江
責任編輯／王躍平
發 行 人／蔡森明
出 版 者／大展出版社有限公司
社　　址／台北市北投區（石牌）致遠一路2段12巷1號
電　　話／（02）28236031・28236033・28233123
傳　　眞／（02）28272069
郵政劃撥／01669551
網　　址／www.dah-jaan.com.tw
E - mail ／ service@dah-jaan.com.tw
登 記 證／局版臺業字第2171號
承 印 者／傳興印刷有限公司
裝　　訂／眾友企業公司
排 版 者／弘益電腦排版有限公司
授 權 者／山西科學技術出版社
初版1刷／2017年（民106）6月

定　價／350元

大展好書　好書大展
品嘗好書　冠群可期